By the same author

TALK OF PROPAGANDA
THE TECHNIQUE OF PERSUASION
ARMS AND TOMORROW

TO FALL LIKE LUCIFER

To fall
like Lucifer

Ian Harvey

'And when he falls, he falls like Lucifer,
Never to hope again.'

SHAKESPEARE, *Henry VIII*

SIDGWICK & JACKSON

LONDON

First published in Great Britain May 1971
by Sidgwick and Jackson Limited

Copyright © Ian Harvey 1971

Reprinted June 1971

ISBN 0 283.48463.2

Printed in Great Britain by Whitefriars Press Ltd
London & Tonbridge for
Sidgwick and Jackson Limited
1 Tavistock Chambers, Bloomsbury Way
London, W.C.1

*To those in peril on the sea —
and elsewhere.*

CONTENTS

Prologue

To regret one's own experience is to arrest one's development.

OSCAR WILDE

THE writing of autobiographies is a dangerous practice. If they are true they often reveal, sometimes unintentionally, aspects of a man's character which he has long been at pains to conceal. If they are untrue the writer could well be better employed on a work of more exciting fiction.

This therefore is not an autobiography in the fullest sense of the word: such things are reserved in any case for celebrities and criminals. There are many aspects of it which are autobiographical and there are others which constitute a personal commentary on the controversial and complex subject of homosexuality. Some people may feel that in the circumstances it contains things better left unwritten. I did in fact hesitate for some time before setting them down on paper.

I finally decided to do so, not for the sake of publicity of which I have had enough, but because so much has been written and said about homosexuality and homosexuals that is ignorant and pre-judiced nonsense. Whether people like it or not they cannot help the way they are made. Admittedly they are also given the power to control themselves but they do not always make use of it and it is not always completely their fault that they do not.

When this happens they find themselves in trouble with society which often appears to be more concerned with those who break the eleventh commandment – thou shalt not be caught – than it is with the other ten. They become social outcasts, rejected by their friends and derided by their enemies. They feel that they have deprived themselves of the whole purpose of living. Such talents as they possess, and these may be many, can no longer be put to the fullest use. Consequently they become depressed and sink deeper and deeper into the slough of despond and the mire of degradation.

The branded homosexual, although no longer liable to the same punishments as he was in the past, is punished both by society and himself. He is weighed down by shame and guilt; he is pursued by fear of the consequences of his actions to himself and to those whom he loves or for whom he is responsible. In order to try to escape from it all he may resort to drink and drugs. Because he has been rejected by the society to which he once belonged he may well turn against it and seek the companionship of those who have been similarly rejected or who have never belonged. And so he goes from bad to worse. I know all this from personal experience.

For those in public life the disaster is greater than it is for those who are private individuals although the human damage is the same: we are all people. They are fully exposed to the glare of publicity which surrounds their position. If they are tempted to indulge in an agony of self-pity they would do well to remember that, just as public life bears the glittering prizes for those who succeed, so also does it hold the powers of heaviest punishment for those who betray its trust. Although harsh, this is as it should be. Those who bring down the standards of public life will ultimately bring down the society for which they are responsible. I am well aware that those who opposed the reform of the law on homosexuality had this very much in mind and whilst I do not agree with them I respect their reasons.

This is therefore not a book of lamentations; if it were it would not be worth reading and I would have been wrong to have written it. I have learned what it is like to meet with triumph and disaster, in that order, and I do not pretend that I have treated either as an impostor. Nor do I pretend that others who have to endure a similar experience, and I pray that they may be few in number, will draw any particular encouragement from what I have written. All I have tried to do is to convince them that if it happens it is not the end of the world however much it may appear to be so at the time and for many years after. Nor would I insult their intelligence by telling them that time is a great healer because that is just not true.

I have also tried to apply my own experience to a problem which is both human and social and to reach some conclusions without emotion and as objectively as possible. In order to prove my argument I have had to describe in some detail what actually happened to me. This has not been an easy exercise but it has been necessary so that what I have written should be seen to be factual and not merely theoretical.

I have studied with particular care the various reports that have been written on the subject and, in particular, the Report of the Wolfenden Committee which was intelligent and courageous. I do not claim to have the knowledge or the wisdom of those who have written and contributed to them, nor have I had the same access to case histories. But I have the advantage over them, if such it may be called, of personal involvement. Thus I understand at first hand both the human factor and the social reaction.

Because this is not a complete autobiography it is not exact in its chronology. I have endeavoured to maintain a balance between light and shade, and there has been plenty of both. If there are parts which appear too light-hearted it is because I wish to underline, particularly for those who have their difficulties, that it is imperative to retain one's sense of humour.

I could well have divided this book into two parts: the first entitled 'going up' and the second 'coming down'. Such is the nature of the story, as it is indeed the story of many people's lives. The political theme runs through both of them. In the first part it is an account of the days of a practising politician; in the second it becomes merely the expression of views by a spectator of the scene. I thought it relevant to include this detail because it helps to paint the picture. The lesson of it is that there is no escape from politics for the dedicated politician even in exile: it remains for ever on the mind and in the blood-stream. That has been for me an additional punishment.

In some cases I have omitted names of people. This is not because I cannot remember them: I have always had a good memory for names and faces. I have either felt it better not to mention them or I have preferred to treat them as nameless. Many people have shown me great kindness. I have not acknowledged this in a personal way because I know that society, in its kindly way, would jump at the chance of deducing that they too were like me. I shall deny society at least that one pleasure.

Finally this is not an apologia nor is it a justification. It is merely a record of one man's experience. From some it may call forth scorn and from some evoke pity. The first I do not care about and the second I do not require. Nor do I seek approval from those who may, for good or bad reasons, have some sympathy. From the homosexual society I hope I shall receive the tacit acknowledgement that I have treated the subject with justice and with truth. For those of them who have met with similar disaster I have no particular message because each man is his own island. I would, however, say to them that, whilst it is impossible to forget the past it is wise to avoid dwelling upon the future which might have been and now never can be. Sterile dreams putrify the mind and destroy the mental processes. That is the road to further catastrophe.

Many years ago I wrote at the front of my diary the following lines from Shelley whose poetry I greatly admire:

> *To suffer woes which Hope thinks infinite,*
> *To forgive wrongs darker than death or night,*
> *To defy Power which seems omnipotent,*
> *To love and bear: to hope till hope creates*
> *From its own wreck the thing it contemplates –*

I wrote that in the account of my life at a time when for me the future was bright and exciting. It seems an appropriate quotation to put at the beginning of this latter account which is written in somewhat different circumstances. Even on the scrap-heap the sun sometimes shines.

1 *Getting to know People*

If you can talk with crowds and keep your virtue
Or walk with Kings – nor lose the common touch.
RUDYARD KIPLING

MY father was killed in the First World War. He foolishly got
in the way of a bullet outside Kut-el-Amara. When my turn came
to face the foe I was careful not to make the same mistake. My
father was a regular soldier serving in the Indian Army and consequently I was born under the awning of the British Raj. I have
always rather selfishly resented his choice of career as my grandfather had created a number of distilleries in Scotland, the best of
which was on the island of Islay. Had my father gone into the
family business I should undoubtedly have followed him which
would have been highly satisfactory. The road to the isles has always attracted me.

When the war broke out my mother and I returned to England
and went to live with her parents at 4 Marchmont Gardens, Richmond, Surrey, which still stands amongst the debris of modern
development. My father's death was a terrible blow to my mother
and left us practically penniless so that she had to go out to work.

I remember none of these things and I remained oblivious to
the unhappiness which she concealed so successfully from me
although sometimes I would hear her crying at night. Naturally
I took my father's place in her affections and this was at the root
of many problems which were subsequently to beset me. It may
seem ungrateful to state this but it is nevertheless true and I know
that the psychiatrists would agree with me. When, in later years, it

became clear that we were on the verge of another holocaust I was confirmed in my decision not to get married until it was over lest my wife and children should be faced with similar difficulties to those which beset my mother and me. There were also other reasons.

My first vivid recollection of youth was sitting in my push-chair under a tree whilst a German aircraft flew overhead. As I did not know what it was all about I was not afraid although my nurse appeared to be about to collapse. I had a vague idea that the Germans were not nice people, but people who all wore spiked helmets and were always referred to by my grandfather as filthy Huns or dirty Boche. My mother once told me, and I really think she believed it, that if the Germans had won the war we should all have been locked up in prison.

When the war was over we settled down to life in Richmond with walks in the park, fishing for stickle-backs and newts and gathering chestnuts in the autumn. I had a dog called Billy who was a wire-haired terrier whom I loved dearly and who fought with every dog in the neighbourhood; I also had two goldfish, one of which I killed through overfeeding.

My first excursion to the theatre was to see *Where the Rainbow Ends* which was performed annually by the Italia Conti Company at the Holborn Empire. I took an immediate fancy to the Dragon King who was very evil and who wore a marvellous shining green outfit. I was very put out when he was inevitably killed by St. George who was a rather pink and white character in armour with a red cross emblazoned on his tummy. I have no doubt that Freud would have a definite explanation for this perverse reaction which was not shared by the rest of the audience who were all on the side of the right and the good. I came away singing the Dragon King's song, the tune and opening lines of which I can still remember. I was six at the time. I committed a similar misdemeanour the next year when we went to see *Peter Pan* by refusing to clap my hands to show that I believed in fairies as I had taken a dislike to Tinkerbell; I was also highly delighted when Wendy was hit by an arrow as I had taken a dislike to her too. Needless to say I thought Captain Hook was a splendid chap as opposed to Peter Pan who did not really appeal to me as he was a girl. Although these childish events may seem trivial they had some basis in reality.

My mother and my father's relations thought it would be nice if I were to wear a kilt on Sundays and when I went to parties. In the suburban atmosphere in which we lived this caused some amusement. The boys called me a girl and the girls thought I was a cissy. They were all of them keen to know what I wore underneath. Out of this sprang an innate anti-feminine reaction which was to last for many years and was one of the reasons why I never had a girlfriend in my teens. It was not surprising, in these childhood circumstances, that I grew up an insufferable small boy.

When I was nine and a half my mother presented me with a stepfather. This was a grave shock to my system and it took me ten years to get over it; the same applied to him. Any man who marries a woman who has children by another marriage is taking on a task no less difficult than a woman who marries a man in a similar position. If the children are very young then the problems are not so great or, at least, they need not be. I was at the most difficult age as I was neither a child nor sufficiently grown up to appreciate the nature of the situation. I make no excuses for what afterwards transpired except to observe that for once I do not think it was all my fault and that no one did much to help; my stepfather least of all.

Initially I think that this was due to shyness and to a fear of intruding where he was not wanted which showed that he had not thought the matter out. He had no doubt been warned not to rush it; but that did not mean that he had to stand aside, as he did, until things got out of hand. I realised early on that I still had immense influence over my mother, in fact far greater than he had, because for her the image of my father still remained in me. I knew that I had only to make a scene and she would take my side whether I was right or wrong; and I was usually wrong. So I made plenty of scenes at which I became an adept. As I have said I was an insufferable small boy. Again I have no doubt that psychiatrists could say what effect this was to have upon my future make-up.

As a parent and an adult it is easy for me now to look back objectively on the whole scene and I do so without anger or bitterness because it was by no means a long story of darkness and woe. In fact my mother and I were considerable beneficiaries of this somewhat confused marriage, at least in material terms, because my stepfather was not poor. R. J. O. Meyer, that remarkable headmaster of that equally remarkable school, Millfield, which he created almost single-handed, has said that there are no bad child-

ren, only bad parents. This is only a half-truth which I am tempted
to call typical, although it is undeniable that the responsibility for
juvenile development, and juvenile delinquency, rests with the
parents. I would also add that there are also bad teachers and I
have seen them at work in numerous capacities.

When I was eleven I was sent away to a preparatory school which
I deduced was a move on the part of my stepfather to get me out
of the way. If it had been I had no right to blame him. It was not,
of its sort, a bad school. It was run by two men who were more
concerned with making a profit for themselves than with contri-
buting to the educational system of the country. Consequently they
largely employed masters who could not get into university or
who, having got in, came down with inferior degrees or with no
degree at all. One of them took a greater liking to me than he
should have done. This surprised me, as I was not at all an attractive boy.

This was the beginning of my sex education which till that time
had been nil. My mother had never spoken about it to me nor had
my stepfather, and my grandfather had long forgotten all about
it. Consequently when I had my first wet dream I thought I must
have some terrible disease and dared not tell anyone. My sexual
instincts were subsequently titillated by the decision, made on the
advice of the professional nurse who attended the birth of my half-
sister, that I should be circumcised as, being a month premature,
I was too much of a weakling to have it done at birth. This is not
an experience that I would recommend to anyone as it was extremely painful and somewhat embarrassing. It did have the effect
of making me much more conscious of that part of my anatomy.

Apart from this new experience with the master at my prep
school I learned very little. I disliked all games particularly cricket
which, next to Catholicism and golf, was a religion with my stepfather, who had played for Somerset. I was once made to run round
the field three times for stopping the ball with my foot. The fact
that I had stopped it at all was, in my opinion, an achievement. I
have since noted that many of our distinguished cricketers who
have failed to adopt my method have given away at least four runs
as a result. When I told my stepfather of my exploit he was horrified. Needless to say I did not tell him of my experiences with
the master who was teaching me about sex. I introduced the man
to my mother on sports day, who thought he was charming

and thanked him profusely for taking such an interest in me. He did not bat an eyelid. He was Welsh.

It was at this time that the creative spirit of another kind began to stir within me: at least that is how I like to describe my first efforts at poetry, my play, and three rather slim novels. Oddly enough, all of them were totally lacking in any sex interest. I also wrote a short history of the London General Omnibus Company which existed before London Transport took over and wrecked the system. My first novel was all about Sodom and Gomorrah which admittedly as a theme had great potential, but this escaped me. The second was entitled *The Tiger* and was a eulogy on Lenin. This was not thought at all suitable by the masters of a school catering for the sons of successful capitalists.

I put matters right with my play which was all about Imperial Rome. I played the part of Caesar which took up eighty per cent of the performance and two of the boys I didn't like were made to be slaves who were continuously maltreated and ultimately executed. My mother who was in the audience was thrilled and could not make up her mind whether I would end up as Poet Laureate or another John Galsworthy. I was in a similar dilemma.

I established, when I had reached the exalted rank of monitor, a club to which all who valued peace of mind and body, were forced to belong. I cannot remember what it was called but it involved the placing of all toys, games and possessions of entertainment value in a central pool from which they could be taken by any member of the club. This act of open defiance of the capitalist system, unlike my book on Lenin, passed muster with the staff who had come to recognise my powers of making a nuisance of myself, until one of the parents who was very rich complained.

It was at this time that an important event took place which was to re-shape my character and the course of my life. I passed my Common Entrance exam, rather better than most of my so-called mentors had expected, to my father's old school Fettes College in Edinburgh. From that moment on I was to put away childish things and to become a man. I had never been to Scotland and this was an exciting, if somewhat alarming, experience. I shall always remember my arrival at the school on a cold night in January 1928. The lights of Edinburgh were sparkling in the darkness as my train, the *Royal Scot*, approached the capital. It was not normal for new boys, or rather new men, to arrive in the spring term. Accordingly I was looked on with some suspicion. It was assumed that there must be some sinister reason whereas it was merely due to the fact that my prep school had not thought it advisable for me to risk failing the exam in the summer. They may well have been justified in their apprehension but it was not a great tribute to their teaching prowess.

The first evening at supper, which consisted of porridge, thick chunks of bread and very hard cheese at nine o'clock, I sat next to a boy who immediately demanded to know where I lived. I told him London to which he reacted contemptuously with the remark, 'Och, you're a cockney.' This was too much for a resident of the respectable suburb of Richmond, Surrey. I corrected him but he would have none of it nor would any of those present. He concluded the argument by announcing rather grandly, as if it confirmed him as an authority on the subject of people's origins, that he himself came from the top house in Aberarder. I felt it wiser not to observe that I had never heard of the place.

Despite all this display of Scottish pride, to which I personally took no exception, Fettes was regarded by many people, particularly in Edinburgh, as an English school. This was a ridiculous prejudice which emanated from the fact that when the school was founded in 1870 the Trustees sought advice from Uppingham and then appointed an English headmaster, Dr. Potts, who came from Rugby.

Sir William Fettes, a successful Edinburgh business man and twice Lord Provost, directed in his will that 'It is my intention that the residue of my whole estate should form an Endowment for the maintenance, education and outfit of young people whose parents have either died without leaving sufficient funds for that purpose or who, from innocent misfortune during their lives, are unable to give suitable education to their children'. The Trustees in their wisdom thought it appropriate to make arrangements for the inclusion of fee-paying boys. For this they were roundly attacked by the people of Edinburgh and the Scottish press for not carrying out the founder's wishes. One Scottish journalist went so far as to denounce the Fettes Foundationers, who were not fee-paying, as 'sons of decayed princes brought up in conditions of "Sardanapalian luxury"'. As their parents were largely poorly paid ministers of the Church of Scotland the writer would clearly have qualified today for a post on the *Daily Mirror*.

Whilst this mixing of boys with very different backgrounds was wholly right, and well in advance of its time, in the field of education it did lead to difficulties which even in my time had not been completely eliminated. This was largely due to a mistake in administration which resulted in all the Foundation Scholars and Foundationers being segregated in the School House whilst the rest lived in outhouses. Their living conditions were no better and in the winter the walk up to school in rain, snow and sleet was particularly unattractive.

Not surprisingly, the boys in Schoolhouse were generally more intelligent than those in the fee-paying houses. They had to be. They had no rich relations to pay their way for them, no inherited capital to give them a firm base in life, and no family businesses with seats at the boardroom table waiting for them. In the main they were all the better for it. This is not to suggest that they were all successes and that their richer colleagues were all comparative failures. That would be making the sort of foolish assertion of which those who are now determined to destroy the public-school system would undoubtedly approve. In many ways this mixing of the backgrounds of boys at the age of fourteen to eighteen bene-fited both elements and they were not slow to take advantage of it: after all the great majority were Scots or of Scottish origin.

Boys being boys they were unlikely to admit this and the Foun-dation Scholars and Foundationers were branded as 'coolidgers'. The 'coolidgers' retaliated by branding their critics as morons and snobs which some of them certainly were. I found myself in a cross-fire position. My father having been a Fettes boy and having been killed in the war left my mother with inadequate funds to educate me as she would have wished. Fettes, through the gener-osity of Old Fettesians, stepped in and paid the bills not only there but also at my prep school. For this I am eternally grateful. I was accordingly sent to Schoolhouse where I was far less intelligent than most of my colleagues, including the boy from the top house at Aberarder who was two years younger than me and was three forms higher up the school. I am glad to say that this did not worry me nor did the attitude of the boys in the other houses whose home lives were more akin to mine.

But it was to worry my stepfather. One of his best friends had three boys at Fettes. The second, who had been asked to keep an eye on me, became one of my closest friends and he was in one of the outhouses. His first reaction was to demand how it came about that the stepson of such a comparatively rich man should be living at the expense of the school. Confronted by this awkward question my stepfather, instead of declaring the true facts which were that he felt that as Fettes had offered to finance my education and, as I was not his son, he had opted out of this responsibility, immediately offered to pay. This was both illogical and cowardly and was also foolish from a domestic point of view. The offer was turned down politely by Fettes and indignantly by my mother, accompanied by some offensive remarks from my grandparents who disliked my stepfather, partly because he was a Catholic and partly because they had become financially indebted to him. This incident was hardly calculated to improve the situation at home, although, as a result of my Fettes education, I was beginning to see his point of view even if I did not entirely support it. I was still determined to hold on to my commanding position over him so far as my mother's affections were concerned. This I did to the end and he was only sustained by the fact that he was able to transfer his own affections, to a considerable degree, to his daughter, who, although not inclined to play cricket, became a champion golfer.

I can truthfully say that I enjoyed my life at Fettes from the moment I arrived until the moment I left. For this reason, amongst others, my account of it will be very short. Today only the stories of those who suffered the tortures of the damned at school, who were physically and sexually assaulted, who spent their time in a coma through taking drugs, who were in continuous revolt against authority and who were finally expelled, are of any public interest. Today, also, it is fashionable to decry the public schools and to deride their contribution to society. Needless to say I reject this intellectual nonsense which is evidence of the spineless inferiority of too many people who, like the abomination of desolation, are sitting where they ought not. One day, when the backlash develops, they will find themselves in for a nasty tumble. I look forward to being around when that happens.

The public school system, of which Arnold was the great architect, has been based on the teaching of the sense of responsibility, the importance of leadership and of service to others. Above all things it underlines that rights imply duties. This is in sharp contrast to some of the prevailing doctrines of the permissive society which accept the defiance of authority, the disregard for accepted moral standards and, when considered necessary, the resort to violence. Those who seek to destroy such a system had better be quite sure that they have something better to put in its place.

One of the most laughable incidents at Fettes occurred during my first term when our house master, a man who rather fancied himself as being progressively minded, which amounted to swimming naked in the swimming-bath and supporting the Labour Party, spoke seriously to us after prayers one evening. He said that a most unfortunate book on a most unsuitable subject, which he would not mention, had been written about our sister-school, Loretto. What made it even more unsuitable was that it had been written by an Old Lorettonian. Anyone found reading this book would be severely punished. The book was called *Lindsay* by John Connell, whose real name was Jack Connell-Robertson and who later became a great friend of mine. Naturally there was a mad rush to get the book which up to that time no one had heard about. I must admit that there was nothing in it that I did not know about already, but maybe I was an exception. When in after years I told Jack about it he was most grateful to the house master in question and offered to send him a signed copy. By that time I suspect the poor chap was reading *Last Exit from Brooklyn*.

Another incident which I recall was less humorous. I was returning from the Sunday visit to the Episcopalian Church – a dreary experience which sowed the seeds of my ultimate departure from the Church of England – when I was overtaken by a boy from another house who was in a great state of agitation. He was a Canadian by birth and had arrived late in time at Fettes. He was much richer than anyone else and possessed a cine-camera with which he took pictures of the house prefects playing rugger. This did not endear him to his colleagues. He asked me if, as a member of the sixth-form library, I would get him the current copy of *The Spectator*. I willingly agreed although I had no idea what the magazine looked like as I had never read it. I duly went to the library but my search was in vain. I informed my suppliant and thought no more about it.

Subsequently it transpired that there was a letter in it on the subject of the disgraceful conditions of fagging and bullying which prevailed at public schools. The letter had been inspired by the fact that a boy at Sedbergh had committed suicide. The great offence which this letter committed was that it was signed by the boy who had asked me to find *The Spectator* and he had given the name of his house at Fettes.

Whatever had happened to the boy at Sedbergh can have been nothing compared with what then happened to the author of this letter. I do not propose to describe the form of punishment meted out to him because it would have enlightened a qualified member of the Gestapo and it was not at all creditable. The boy left the next day. I think that the *Spectator* owed him at least a year's free issues for the number of readers it obtained in one afternoon. Admittedly I suspect few of them have ever read it since.

Meanwhile my creative spirit was stirring again despite this somewhat philistine atmosphere which, I hasten to state, was not totally without mitigation. In company with the music master, Henry Havergal, a brilliant and sophisticated man who has just retired as the Director of the Scottish Academy of Music, I wrote the libretto for two operettas which were performed before a not unappreciative school. The producer, Geoffrey Sale, subsequently became Headmaster of Bruton and then of Rossall. I was moving in distinguished company at an early age. And that was the way I intended to keep it.

When these two productions were in course of preparation there was some alarm in high places when it was learned that the last Fettesian who embarked on a similar project had been Ian Hay Beith who had secretly altered a number of passages unknown to the presiding staff. The result on the night was a huge success but not with the Headmaster which did not augur well for their future. My mother always used to tell me that Ian Hay was my father's favourite author and that he named me after him. I told him this in later years and he was kind enough to receive the news without too much distress.

As I have already indicated I do not propose to record my schooldays at any great length. They changed the direction of my life and I believe they changed it for good; whatever may have gone wrong since did not have its origins then. I found myself a member of a society in which there was a healthy balance between academic and physical activities. Admittedly there was a certain overemphasis on rugby football which had all the trappings of a religion. Those who did not wear the magenta stockings, the mark of 'Bigside' which constituted the members of the first and second fif-

teens, had little hope of achieving the highest positions of authority. Cultural activities were not frowned upon but they were the
province of the few. Today this has been vastly changed as indeed
has the whole conception of school life everywhere. At that
time we were making progress and that was worthwhile.

This again had an important influence upon me. I was not good
at games but I was ambitious to get on. So I realised that I had
better do something about it. It was the simple lesson of life that
if you want something badly enough and you are prepared to
work for it you can usually get it or most of it. Consequently I
drove myself on to get my magenta stockings and I did and thereafter authority followed on. But it did not turn me into a philistine
as intellectuals might imagine. It did in fact give me greater influence in persuading others to follow more intellectual pursuits.
If a man with magenta stockings thought it was all right then
there must be something in it. Such, at least, was the accepted
theory and those who understand the psychology of the herd will
know that this was a normal reaction.

I caused a certain stir in what was officially a non-denominational
school by making contact with the Jesuits. It all started when
Cardinal Bourne re-consecrated the Catholic cathedral in Edinburgh. The colour, the pageantry and the emotional excitement of
the ceremony contrasted vividly with the dreary mutterings of the
Episcopalians. I had already become an Anglo-Catholic for many
of the same reasons, although I had a feeling that it was an
attempt to get the best of both worlds. I had never been tempted
to join the members of the school who attended the Church of
Scotland although it had been the religion of my fathers in so far
as they had one. Sometimes the unhappy boys returned as late as
one-fifteen for Sunday lunch; even the cold repast must have been
a refreshment after the morning's endurance test of lengthy ser-
mons and unending self-invented prayers.

Father Eustace Dudley, who was head of the Jesuit community,
was a dynamic man who was fully prepared to meet the brickbats
of a somewhat anti-Catholic capital with its memories of Mary
Queen of Scots. He possibly went a little too far when in later
years he described the sects in the other churches as insects: but he
had been sorely tried. At my request my mother wrote to the Headmaster, Dr. Alec Ashcroft, asking permission for me to go 'up
town' on Sunday afternoons for instruction. To his credit, for he

was a low-Church man, he agreed, although I think he suspected that Father Eustace Dudley was not the only person I wanted to see.

He had no cause for concern. My discussions, which went on for over a year, came to nothing for the time being. But there was one interesting development. Father Gille, who also instructed me, was expelled from the Jesuits for writing a book on Church unity. I make no claim to have been in any way responsible, although it would have been quite an achievement for a sixteen-year-old schoolboy.

I had originally intended to go to Cambridge as, owing to the influence of Dr. Ashcroft, who was a distinguished Cambridge man and a rugger blue, many Fettesians went there. The wise Henry Havergal thought I was an Oxford type. I think he was right, although I am not sure that I knew what he meant or that I could accurately define the difference between the two universities. My only knowledge of inter-university activities was the Boat Race, which, while I was at school, Oxford never won. Nevertheless I always wore a dark blue rosette and I have worn one ever since in one capacity or another.

I actually went to Cambridge to take my 'little go', which academically was a very apt description. It was then decided that I should try for a scholarship in English. This was largely done to keep me mentally employed during my last year and the only justification for the decision was that I had won a large number of governors' prizes for English verse and English essays. This again I achieved largely because no one else entered. I chose King's and St. Catherine's as my alternatives. Not surprisingly neither of them chose me. My form master, who shared Henry Havergal's view and was also an Oxford man, suggested I should also put in for Christ Church which I did.

So off I went to Christ Church where the result was the same as at Cambridge except that the Junior Censor, Bobby Longden, a man of infinite culture and charm who was killed by a bomb when he was Headmaster of Wellington, was particularly pleasant. He said that if I would like to come up to Christ Church I could do so and that I would not have to take any further exam. I accepted with alacrity not only because I was never much good at exams but also because the spirit of Christ Church had already enthralled me and will continue to do so until the end of my life.

It may seem strange to those who manage to reach the end of this book that I have said nothing about the homosexual side of school life at Fettes and my own involvement with it. I have not made this omission in order to protect an establishment for which I have so great an affection. The fact is that homosexual practice was almost non-existent, compared with what one has heard of other schools.

It has always been one of the common arguments against public schools that they are segregated communities where homosexuality is bound to develop just as in monasteries, nunneries, on board ship and in prisons. In the past the critics did not hesitate to agree nevertheless that homosexual offenders should be sent to prison, which somewhat undermined their case.

We all had our particular friendships and some were admittedly strong enough to be called love. There were, of course, occasions when homosexual activities occurred but they were very much in private. It was regarded as effeminate and effeminacy in our eyes was degrading. Occasionally there were waves of such exploratory ventures as mutual masturbation. My house master, not the progressive one, who was a man of considerable common sense and essentially a man of the world, was approached in a state of great excitement by the head of the house who had uncovered some exploits of this kind. He merely remarked, 'My dear fellow, it's no worse than blowing your nose.' This was very advanced thinking in the early 'thirties and I suspect it would have shocked the Headmaster had he heard about it. It was a great consolation to me, as I was still not certain what terrible damage I might in fact be doing to myself. From a physical point of view I need not have worried.

Mentally I was never deeply involved in a homosexual way whilst I was at school. I suppose that this was largely due to my interests in other directions such as the debating society, the music club and the literary society which were largely my brain-children, and also to the fact that I was not a boy who was either sought after when I was small or looked up to when I was bigger. I had my feelings towards other boys from time to time, but I controlled them. Possibly I was too ill-informed or too frightened to do anything about them.

The one exception was the son of my stepfather's best friend, which had its humorous side. Whilst we were at school we went no distance. In a strange sort of way I think he felt, as he had been told to look after me, that this would have been a breach of trust. I admit that this disappointed me at the time as, in view of subsequent events, I am sure it did him. I was particularly irritated when he asked me to assist him in forming a friendship with another boy in my house who was particularly good-looking. I was at least successful in frustrating that little enterprise. I was quite surprised to have to admit to myself that the reason for this was jealousy.

So up I went to Oxford on Cambridge 'little go' which struck me as a particularly catholic thing to do. Actually the catholicity was theirs not mine. Fettes kindly gave me an exhibition which they divided between me and my best friend who went up to Cambridge. So everyone was happy and honour, albeit of a very lowly order, was satisfied. I arrived at Oxford in the same year as Hitler became Chancellor of Germany, not that there was any great significance in that. It meant, however, that the storm-clouds had not yet appeared, life was full and exciting and the future seemingly unthreatened.

Although I had made my scholarship attempts at English I had decided to read history. The English school at Oxford at that time was generally considered inferior. This may not be a just criticism but I must admit that I never met anyone who was reading English except some rather dreary women. I could not have had a more distinguished team of tutors at Christ Church. They were J. C. Masterman, Keith Feiling, Noel Myres and Patrick Gordon-Walker. For their part I doubt if they ever had a more disappointing pupil but they were all very nice about it, although they did occasionally suggest I should try reading a book or two. Those were the days when it was possible to be more concerned with extra-academic and even extra-mural studies, if you were not aspiring to high academic honours. Today I should have been sent down at the end of a year. The purists would say 'and a good job too' but I am not certain that they would be right.

I remained convinced, especially since looking at Oxford as it is today, that the most important aspect of university life is to learn how to live. This is not the same thing as living it up, as some people appear to believe. Those who have found time to do this have subsequently been a greater asset to society and to themselves than those who have spent their days poring over their books. Although this applies to a lesser degree to the academic profession, those who have become dons and schoolmasters have been far better equipped as a result of not being over-studious, to hand on their message to their pupils.

After the success of my school operettas which were entitled, incidentally, *Bribery and Corruption* and *Prometheus Unwound*, my first thought was to join the O.U.D.S. This I did. Felix Felton was President and the society was flourishing. I also joined the Oxford Union where Michael Foot was in the chair. He was then a Liberal. At that moment I had no politics. I had not intended to continue playing rugger at Oxford. I had failed to get my first fifteen cap at Fettes which had annoyed me. It was a particularly splendid cap with a silver tassel. I was therefore somewhat astonished to receive a card from the Secretary of the Oxford University Rugby Football Club informing me that I had been selected for a 'freshman's trial'. If a cap had been awarded for that I would have jumped at it. As it was I was badly out of training and not nearly good enough. I rushed round to the Secretary, Derrick Lorraine, who had been at Glenalmond, and told him I wanted to withdraw. But he would have none of it. So play I did and was very nearly sick at half-time. It was not surprising that I was not asked to play for the University again. But the damage was done and Christ Church made it clear that it would be regarded as highly disloyal to the College if I did not play for them. My Fettes upbringing forced my hand. 'The House', which is the proper name for Christ Church, so often inaccurately described outside Oxford as Christ-church College, was essentially a rowing college packed with 'Old Etonians' and 'blues'. The rugger men were looked upon as rough philistines, if they were looked upon at all. In my time we had two internationals, three blues and a number of people on the fringe of 'blues'. In my second year we nearly won 'cuppers'. We became a force to reckoned with in the college in more senses than one. For me this provided a break from my political activities, my performance with the O.U.D.S. and my occasional excursions into the realms of history.

The Union intrigued me. It was under a cloud in high places as in the summer of 1933, which was the term before I went up, it had passed the notorious resolution 'That this house will not fight for King or Country'. It has been seriously suggested that as a result of this Ribbentrop assured Hitler that the youth of Britain was too yellow to fight. In fact what the resolution implied was that under the conditions of the time the old nationalistic cry 'For King and Country' was not sufficient reason in itself to justify taking up arms. Had it been worded 'This house does not endorse the slogan "my country right or wrong" ' it would have been similarly passed but no one would have cared. Matters were made worse by Randolph Churchill who, with a characteristic lack of judgement, tried to have the resolution rescinded. He was not any longer an undergraduate nor had he held office in the Union. The members of the Boat Club joined in the fray and raided the debating hall and tore the page from the book. They would have been far better employed practising for the Boat Race which as usual they lost to Cambridge by a large number of lengths.

I made my maiden speech five weeks after arriving and I received a complimentary note from Michael Foot which I have kept. For some strange reason he never sent me one after any of my speeches when we were both members of the House of Commons; but by then he was no longer a Liberal. The last week of term Michael gave me my first 'paper speech'. The motion was that 'Borstal and Eton are a couple of fine old schools'. As a result of my speech I was asked to call on the proctors as I had made an offensive joke about the 'bulldogs' who were their marshals. Actually I had never met one and I never spoke to one throughout my university career. I assured them that I was certain that all 'bulldogs' were splendid people. They thanked me for my courtesy, we doffed caps and the incident was closed. If an undergraduate were sent for by the proctors today for making an offensive remark in the Union I have no doubt that there would be a 'sit-in', a couple of 'demos' and a demand that the Vice-Chancellor should immediately resign in the interests of free speech. Despite being censored for this seemingly revolutionary act I had joined the Conservative Association and I have remained a member of the Party ever since.

Although it was becoming clear to me that politics was the road for me I still had dramatic leanings. I wrote a one-act play which was selected by the O.U.D.S. for performance. It was very bad and I can't remember what it was about. There were many members of the society who were far more dedicated to the theatre than I was. I was content with small parts and I was joined in this by Dennis Price and together we ran on, spoke our few lines, and ran off again. Unlike myself he was not content with such roles in the days that lay ahead.

Peter Glenville was President of the O.U.D.S. during its centenary year. He played Hamlet in the New Theatre which had just been opened. Nevill Coghill directed. The performance became somewhat confused by the system he devised of having soliloquies from separate platforms which were floodlit whilst the rest of the stage was in darkness. Unfortunately those concerned were not in command of the lighting system nor of the machinery which drew curtains backwards and forwards. This tended to upset the actors although Glenville ploughed through it all with courage. It was also unfortunate that John Gielgud was performing Hamlet in London at the same time and comparisons were naturally made. But Glenville ploughed through these as well. At the centenary dinner James Agate was the guest of honour. He paid tribute to Glenville by remarking, 'When I saw you, Mr. President, I could not help remembering your dear parents'. They were Shaun Glenville and Dorothy Ward, who were both brilliant comedians. No one knew how to react, which was what Agate intended. He was definitely my type of man. I laughed.

Glenville ran into trouble of a different kind in the summer with the production of *Richard III*. I shall always remember him upside-down on the steps of Christ Church cloisters. Leontine Sagan produced and Nancy Price played the star female part. This resulted in a far more violent conflict than the battle of Bosworth Field. Miss Sagan took particular delight in cutting large chunks out of Miss Price's speeches. It was announced that Max Reinhardt had invited the company to appear at Salzburg. In fact no such invitation had been issued. When it was necessary to announce this Glenville gave as the reason the danger inherent in the Austrian political situation. The Anschluss had not then taken place. The Austrian Ambassador immediately called on the Foreign Office and a fracas ensued as it was felt that this was a threat to the Austrian tourist trade. So the O.U.D.S. ended up in the rain in Regent's Park. Leontine Sagan retired from the direction and Nancy Price took over and put back all the cuts in her speeches. It was all a good insight into the life of the theatre for those who had chosen it. It confirmed my feeling that, fun though it was, it was not for me. On a subsequent political occasion A. P. Herbert whom I had been supporting as candidate for the university seat called

me 'the C. B. Cochrane of Oxford politics' which I regarded as a
very great compliment then and I still do.

We were a happy crowd at Oxford in my day. None of us
thought we ought to have a hand in running the University. In
fact if this had been suggested we would have taken the view that
it was an attempted dodge of responsibility by those who were
paid to look after us so that we could enjoy life, and the more
serious of us could learn something. Possibly we were irresponsible. We deserved to be. We had a war in front of us and more
responsibility than we had ever envisaged.

My closest friend at Oxford was William Shebbeare who I am
certain, had he lived, would have played a prominent part in the
affairs of the Labour Party. We shared a room in Tom Quad in
Christ Church and at one time I was President of the Oxford
University Conservative Association and he was Chairman of the
Labour Club. The committees met in our rooms and on one occasion we ate the Labour Club's tea. It was all a mistake but they
did not believe it. Were we not profit-grabbing capitalists whose
greatest ambition it was to steal the tea off the workers' table? Bill,
like so many other representatives of the working class, was at
Winchester.

We were looked after by one of the most distinguished scouts
in Christ Church, 'Hicks'. He was a true blue Conservative who
not only deplored Bill Shebbeare but regarded me as a secret
Socialist. This is a view that has been erroneously held by numerous
people since. Bill was killed in the war like many of those who
had said that they would not fight for King and Country. One of
my saddest experiences today is to look at the Christ Church war
memorial which is set in the wall at the entrance to the Cathedral.
On it is written the names of so many friends, members of a generation we could ill afford to lose.

Relationships between the undergraduates, who were never
called students, and the graduates were nearly always cordial. The
most remarkable of Christ Church personalities was R. H. Dundas,
known to all as D. At the risk of repeating a well-known story
I record the occasion at Parsons' Pleasure where he was the great
high priest. Two women undergraduates passed through in a punt
which was strictly against the rules—at least it was in those days.
There was a mad rush by the naked assembly who wrapped their
towels around their waists. D put his towel round his head. When

the alarm was over he was asked about his unorthodox procedure. He replied, 'In Oxford most people recognise me by my face'.

Another visitor at Parsons' Pleasure was Dick Crossman, who with G. D. H. Cole and Patrick Gordon-Walker was one of the trinity which stimulated Socialism amongst the undergraduates. One of the weaknesses of the Conservatives was the fact that no senior members of the University did anything to assist them. In due course we put this right. In Oxford the Conservative graduates were not so much members of the stupid party as the lazy party.

The Catholic community was illuminated by the presence of Father Martin D'Arcy, Master of Campion Hall. Largely due to his energies the new building was established and furnished with taste and at some cost to the faithful. The foundation stone was laid by Julian Asquith, the Earl of Oxford and Asquith, who was usually in such a daze that I was surprised he did not let it fall on his foot. Equal lustre was provided at the Catholic chaplaincy nearby by Ronald Knox. It is a tribute to both these men that they never used their undoubted influence to convert undergraduates to the Faith. We called this area of Oxford the 'quatier Latin'.

It was at Campion Hall that an amusing incident occurred when Hilaire Belloc addressed the Society for Reunion. He had mistakenly thought, as the meeting was taking place in a Catholic institution, that it must be a Catholic society. It was in fact Anglo-Catholic. At the end of the meeting Canon Gooch of Christ Church, who was in the audience, addressed the meeting at some length, although all that was required of him was a question. Many questioners at meetings make the same error and it is the duty of efficient chairmen to curb them. The chairman on this occasion was far from efficient being a pipe-smoking young man with glasses who was said to change his coloured pullovers according to the colour of the feast. Canon Gooch concluded his oration with a waspish demand in a high-pitched voice which students of Christ Church had had to endure on Sundays over the years, 'And what has Mr. Belloc to say to that?' There was then a long silence at the end of which the Chairman plucked up courage to repeat the question to the great genius. Belloc replied, 'I haven't listened to a word he's said.' He had this in common with the majority of the members of Christ Church. After that the meeting collapsed and

Father D'Arcy led the visitor away to more congenial conditions and a glass of port.

It was at the Chaplaincy that I first met Harold Macmillan who was the main speaker at the debate at which I contested the Presidency. He and Ronnie Knox were close friends. Many years later I accompanied Harold Macmillan as a junior Minister to Ronnie's funeral service at Westminster Cathedral when the panegyric was beautifully preached by Martin D'Arcy. It was, I think, the first time that a Prime Minister had been present in the Cathedral.

Ronald Knox was undoubtedly one of the finest ex-Presidential speakers in Union debates – especially at Eights Week when humour was the order of the night. Those who spoke on the other side and who had taken insufficient care to prepare were totally eclipsed. This was undoubtedly good for their souls if not for their egos. One of those whose soul and ego were not so affected was Hannen Swaffer. He came to speak at the Union shortly after Ronnie had been made a monsignor. He was talking to me before dinner when Canon Claude Jenkins of Christ Church appeared. Swaffer broke off in the middle of a sentence and rushed forward crying, 'My dear Monsignor, congratulations on your elevation to the purple.' This was not well received by the distinguished though distinctly Protestant cleric. After the debate, at which Swaffer made a thoroughly deplorable speech, he sat next to me again as by that time I was the only one whose powers of endurance were still intact. He said to me, 'People say to me, Harvey, what, my dear Swaffer, is the secret of your great command of the platform?' To which I foolishly replied, 'And what do you say?' At the end of the next half-hour my powers of endurance were no longer intact. Fortunately it was time to go to bed. I reached the conclusion that the best platform for him was the one at Oxford Station – the up-side for Paddington.

Shortly after Ronald Knox became a monsignor he arrived at Brompton Oratory for the Duke of Norfolk's wedding. He was in full regalia which he seldom wore. A voice from the crowd cried out, 'Hot from Rome', to which he replied, 'No, cold from Oxford'. He should undoubtedly have been made a Bishop; a more intelligent hierarchy would have seen to it. When I left Oxford I went to say good-bye to him. It was practically the last thing I did there. He presented me with a copy of his latest thriller entitled *Double Cross Purposes*. In it he had written : 'Dedicated to Ian Harvey in the hope that (during four years' residence at Oxford) he has learned the secret none can utter and the certainty that he will tell it when he goes down.' How right he was.

During my time at Oxford I was selected to represent the undergraduate element at the Harvard Tercentenary Celebrations in 1936. It was a great experience which I thoroughly enjoyed and I came to have a great admiration and respect for the American people which I still retain. I had to make several speeches and the charm of it was that one could dig up all the old jokes which one would never have dared to do at home, although I have known speakers who have taken that risk and got away with it because their audiences were too polite. The American undergraduates enjoyed funny speeches, although, in the main, they were addicted to making serious ones. I caused confusion to my neighbours when I asked for a glass of port before speaking, a habit I had got into at Oxford, although I don't really like port. Someone told me that it steadies the nerves and any speaker who is not nervous before making a major speech is almost bound to be a bad speaker. After a wild hunt one was produced – in fact it was a whole bottle. My neighbour was a delightful Cambridge professor called Merryman who was on loan to Harvard. He told me he had never been able to get port at dinners and that this was a real achievement. Whilst I was speaking he disposed of half the bottle, and it was not a very long speech.

President Roosevelt was the guest of honour at the final day's ceremonies. I was greatly shocked by the ill-mannered way in which he was received. Admittedly they were mostly Republicans, but he was the President of the United States of America and there were many like myself who were foreigners in the assembly. I decided there and then that had I been an American I would have been a Democrat. Now after Eisenhower and Nixon I am even more convinced. Roosevelt was unperturbed. It was a wet day and we sat in the open in the pouring rain on red cushions from which the dye came off on our coats. This, said the President, was his way of soaking the rich. They all laughed at that but in a somewhat restrained way.

When I was in America I learned about the Edward VIII affair. The British press by general agreement, and with commendable self-restraint, had kept this very quiet. There had, of course, been the pictures of the cruise on the yacht *Nalin* and in the upper

B

circles, in which I did not move, a great deal was known or invented. The subsequent events which led to the abdication four months later have been fully recorded and views expressed on both sides. At Oxford there was strangely little reaction one way or the other.

When it actually happened my mind went back to the night when George V died. I was in my rooms in 2 Brewer Street, Oxford, and Tom, the Christ Church bell, tolled away into the early hours. It was the end of an era for those of us who thought of the monarchy in terms of King George and Queen Mary. I remembered also how, two days later, the cross fell off the crown on top of the coffin as the procession wended its way to Westminster Hall. King Edward picked it up; he was after all *fidei defensor*. I recalled his first speech to the nation with its slightly uncouth accent, so different from the gruff tones of his father. Finally I listened to that last speech with its slightly uncontrolled cry of 'God save the King'. I was strangely unmoved. For me the monarchy meant more than the man. Quite obviously I had become a true Conservative.

The abdication was a crisis for the monarchy. Apart from the issues of the morganatic marriage, divorce and politics, it brought the throne into the field of controversy which it had evaded on any major question since the four Georges. It made clear to those in authority that the society of the 'thirties was no longer totally composed of loyal and obedient subjects. In addition Edward VIII's remark about something being done for the unemployed in Wales was interpreted by some as an indication not so much of a king who cared as of a king who intended to interfere. The last two kings who tried to do that ended their respective careers on the scaffold and in exile. There is no doubt that Baldwin fully understood all that; it would have been ridiculous if he had not. The suggestion that this was the governing impulse in his handling of the abdication crisis is not borne out by the facts. It was the King himself who made it inevitable by his refusal to accept the responsibilities inherent in his job. There is some reason to believe that he misled himself over the power of his enormous popularity when he was Prince of Wales. Henry V made no such mistake as poor Falstaff was soon made to understand. George VI saved the situation by returning to the traditional conduct of his father and, with the coming of the war, the issue was submerged.

I have embarked upon this divergence because it is intriguing for us of the generation who went through it all to be asked who the Duke of Windsor is; few know who Mrs. Simpson was or is and even fewer care. Had they been alive at the time their reaction would no doubt have been very different and we could well have become a republic by now. As it was Oxford took the whole thing very calmly mainly because it happened out of term and Christmas was coming.

The time came for me to take Schools. I did badly as I expected I would as I had spent too much time on other things. I was not particularly worried as I had got myself a job with an advertising agency. In those days very few advertising men had good degrees; in fact very few advertising men had been to a university. The man who persuaded me to take this course was David Ogilvy, whose 'fag' I had been at school. He had been up at Oxford and at Christ Church but had departed after a term and went to work in a kitchen in a Paris hotel. Today he is one of the most successful men in advertising and one of the few British advertising executives to succeed on Madison Avenue. At that time he was a junior executive with Mather and Crowther of which his brother Francis was the Managing Director. Today it is called, as one might expect, Ogilvy and Mather.

This is not the place to enter into a long discussion on the subject of the functions of advertising. This has been done by numerous people, in fact I have myself written two books on the subject. I became an advertising man because I was interested in people, because I set great store by the task of communicating with them and because I regarded it as an important and exciting job. I still believe all these things. I also regarded it as the sort of job which I could do at the same time as being a politician because that was what I had decided to become.

Since I joined Mather and Crowther in the autumn of 1937 advertising has developed in many different directions. Its social implications and its power as part of the machinery of communication are a subject for study in themselves.

At Mather and Crowther in 1937 there were two schools of thought prevailing in the agency. There was the older generation who were lambasted in the book *Savoy Grill 1.30*. This was probably the most successful anti-advertising propaganda produced in the 'thirties and was largely responsible for the image of advertising in the minds of people outside the craft. It was at the Savoy Grill that advertising men sold their ideas to their clients over martinis and lunch. The bigger the lunch the greater the chance of success. The younger generation rejected the philosophy of hunches over lunches. They were influenced by the American school where advertising was both more advanced and more respected and concerned themselves with such matters as human and mass psychology, creativity, marketing and the techniques of communication.

I found myself in an intriguing position. I was the protégé of the Ogilvys who believed in the American approach and they were undoubtedly right. On the other hand I was a personal friend of Gordon Boggon, the Vice-Chairman, one of the great advertising personalities of his day, who belonged to the older generation. And he was by no means all that wrong. He was a far warmer character than the Ogilvys and he was much closer to the ordinary people who had a great affection for him. He was moreover highly successful and was responsible at that time for a high percentage of the firm's turnover. He could not be dismissed out of hand and he had no intention of being dismissed. There was not much love lost between the two camps and because I had sympathies with both I came to be known as the mutual friend. Although there were disagreements there was an immense amount of animation and it was by no means the break from university life that existed in more respectable and professional businesses. I have never regretted my decision to become an advertising man. No one can stop me being that even if I have only myself to advertise.

At an early stage I was sent off on attachment to one of our main clients, Genatosan, makers of Sanatogen, Genasprin, Genozo toothpaste and proprietary brands of medicinal products including Cystopurin which performed miracles for those who had bladder complaints. One of the first slogans to ring in my ears, in fact it still rings, was 'At any time of strain or pain, Genasprin sees you through.' It did. Which all goes to prove the importance of truth in advertising.

The headquarters of Genatosan was at Loughborough which was not as flourishing a town then as it is now, nor nearly so well known. The Loughborough Colleges as such did not exist. I was placed under the supervision of the Sales Manager, Mr. Blackwell, a dynamic little man to whom I took a great liking, primarily because he knew his job and there were so many people around who did not. This liking was not immediately mutual since he assumed that as an Oxford graduate and an advertising man, which he regarded as a strange combination, I would never want to do a stroke of work and, in any case, would not know how to. I soon disillusioned him.

One of my most comical, and unprofessional, jobs at Loughborough which Mr. Blackwell entrusted me with when he had discovered that I could not only work but also write was to compose the letters for the firm's doctor in reply to people who wrote in asking how best to make use of Genatosan products or who complained about them. A popular subject was the affliction of the bladder for which the redoubtable Cystopurin was the all-time remedy. My slogan 'Trouble with your urine — take Cystopurin' was not thought entirely ethical by Mr. Blackwell, although I had some difficulty in preventing him from sending it to Mather and Crowther for their consideration.

On Saturday mornings the doctor, who was a local G.P., would come in to write his letters. This normally took him all morning, but with my assistance he was able to arrive at eleven-thirty and leave at noon having signed his mail with hardly a glance. Had I been about to be dismissed I could have had enormous fun; I suspect he would have been dismissed too and probably summoned by the General Medical Council. But I resisted the temptation. I was obviously developing that sense of responsibility which had never bothered me much at Oxford. For this I have to thank Mr. Blackwell.

After three months at Loughborough I was sent out on the road to learn how to sell. Even at that stage Mr. Blackwell was slightly nervous. I was given the Sheffield area which proved to be an interesting coincidence as I was soon to become the prospective Conservative candidate for Don Valley. For some odd reason the tough Yorkshire chemists decided to take pity on the green trainee salesman. During my first month on the road I sold nearly twice as much as my predecessor, but he had admittedly been sacked for idleness. Having no home to go back to at nights I was ready to spend more time on the job which was, for me, a novelty. My tour of duty ended at the same time as the annual salesmen's conference. At this Mr. Blackwell took particular pleasure in pointing out my achievements to the regular members of his staff. I nearly came to a sticky end after the dinner that night. Genatosan were kind enough to invite me to join their company but I said that I had an obligation to Mather and Crowther, which was true. At the same time it was an experience which stood me in good stead in the future. So back I came to London. It was the spring of 1938 and the year of Munich.

Despite the bold face we all put on most of us were pretty certain by Christmas 1938 that it was unlikely to be a Happy New Year. I was by that time the prospective Conservative candidate for Don Valley and I felt that it was my duty, in so far as I had any real duty, to try to reassure people; but I was far from being reassured myself. I suppose that could be judged as political dishonesty but I took the line that if that was the way my leader wanted to play it I also should play it that way. Others disagreed and many others professed afterwards to have disagreed. That is human nature.

I decided I had better do something about it, so I joined the Territorial Army. I hated soldiering and had been a distinct failure in the school O.T.C. as it was then called. What my Regular Army father would have said about it I shall never know.

George Harvie Watt, now Sir George Harvie-Watt, was the M.P. for Richmond and was a family friend. He commanded a Territorial regiment in Merton and Morden. It had once been the 6th City of London Rifles, but had been converted under the Hore-Belisha era to Royal Engineers and moved out to the suburbs where recruitment was better. I became Sapper Harvey. I knew nothing at all about engineering and nor did anyone else except Harvie Watt. We were engaged in the highly dangerous task of manning searchlights. As we had very little equipment at that stage I learned very little about them either, which suited me very well. Unlike some of my friends who joined the Guards and were nearly battered to death on the square I was all set for a quiet start in the war if it came or, more properly, when it came. In the spring of 1939 I was granted a commission. I was totally unfitted to command men in the field. Fortunately for them I never did, so most of them survived.

We went to camp in July and returned in the middle of August. A fortnight later we were recalled for duty from which we were not released for six years. This was the end of the world that I and all my friends had known and in which we had fun. It was the

beginning of six years of darkness when much of one generation
was obliterated and a whole new one grew up under depressing
conditions, deprived of the legitimate pleasures of youth and exposed to danger and to death. Their subsequent survival has been
a tribute to their stamina and to that of those who looked after
them. It has also had in it the seeds of violence and of mistrust
which still remain in the life-blood of the nation.

The regular Adjutant of the Regiment was withdrawn shortly
after we were really at war, if such a phrase can be used for our
quiet sojourn in Sussex. Harvie Watt made me Adjutant which
pleased no one except him and me and, so far as I was concerned,
that was all that mattered for the time being. I started badly in my
relationship with higher military authority. The Brigade Major, a
humourless man and a Regular soldier who detested Territorial
soldiers because he felt that having to deal with them lowered his
status, sent all the regiments an important message concerning
attacks by enemy aircraft. It was marked 'Top Secret' and it read :
'They may fly high or they may fly low', to which I sent back the
message: 'What happens if they fly in between?' This might have
been thought funny in the Oxford Union, or even in the House of
Commons but it did not amuse Brigade. I learned my lesson and
I also had my first introduction to the flood of meaningless jargon
which was to flow across the lines of communication for endless
days and nights to come.

It was not until Dunkirk that the peace and quiet of our existence was disturbed. Our headquarters were at Plumpton Place
under the lip of the South Downs and near the race course. I suspected that this was very likely to be the exact area where the invasion would come. Subsequent documents concerning 'Sea Lion'
have proved that I was right. Harvie Watt and I toured the land
defences from Hythe to Brighton. When we got back we decided that the only thing to do was to have a couple of large double
Scotches and to go to bed with loaded revolvers readily available.
But the invasion did not come and it was just as well that it did
not. Once they had established a firm bridge-head I reckon that
Hitler's tanks would have got to London quicker than the
Brighton Belle.

The bombing of London during the following months put a
severe strain on the morale of our men; not because they were
seriously in action but because they were in the safety of the fields

whilst their wives and families, those who had not been evacuated, were in the area over which the sky was deadly red. It was no wonder that some went absent without leave and it was hard to punish them for doing so. My stepfather had fled to Bournemouth, much against my mother's wishes, and this made me feel bad when it came to dealing with men whose families had remained at home. It brought home to me the meaning of total war.

Our life was temporarily enlivened by a dramatic move by the War Office which had never before had war so close to its own doorstep. A fleet of London taxis was commandeered and despatched to assist with our mobility. The drivers, who were all Londoners, arrived in a convoy at Godstone at five o'clock on a summer morning. They were in high spirits and immediately found kindred spirits amongst the men. As we were now highly military-minded it was obvious to us that there was no point in having mobility without armament. We therefore decided to mount machine-guns, which we possessed, in the taxis and for this purpose we cut holes in the sides and backs. We also issued the drivers with uniforms which delighted them but not the Quarter-Master General. He was even less delighted when, on their return to London after a month in the country, they demanded to be reimbursed for repairing their taxis. I suspect the debate was still going on when the war ended.

At about this time we were converted from the Royal Engineers to the Royal Artillery. This made sense as we were involved in the same operation as the gunners and had nothing whatever to do with the sappers. This was a matter of great distress to Harvie Watt who was a real 'sapper' and enjoyed his mess nights with people dancing round him singing 'Hurrah for the C.R.E.' whilst he had a lighted bowl of brandy on his head. Owing to the exigencies of the service we converted this to methylated spirit. I found this all rather ridiculous but then I found all such mess-night performances tedious in the extreme. He was relieved of his agony shortly afterwards and promoted to Brigadier. This post he held for only a short time as he was sent for by Winston Churchill and made his P.P.S. which must have been every bit as dangerous as engaging the enemy.

I too was promoted a year later and became Brigade Major of an A.A. Brigade in Harrow, part of which territory was one day to become my constituency. I was warned that my Brigade

Commander, Brigadier T. Carleton Harrison was a fire-eater and that few members of his staff lasted for long. I quickly discovered that this was a myth and I formed a friendship which was to last until his death long after the war. He was a formidable person to look at and his subordinates were terrified of him. This was unjustified but I did nothing to disillusion them as it made it easier for me to deal with them. Some of them were not very bright and had to be sent away to less onerous tasks. In some cases this was more my doing than his but I never admitted this; it would in any case have been both presumptuous and disloyal. One such case was the Colonel who after the Brigadier had thumped on the table and announced, 'I'm from Missouri', remarked, 'Really, sir, I thought you lived in Cheam.' It was clear to me that this was a man who did not possess the necessary qualifications for responsible command.

Our headquarters was situated close to the headquarters of Anti-Aircraft Command. As a result of a visit to a mess night, which was particularly successful, by the Major-General General Staff, Major-General R. F. Whitaker, I was appointed G.S.O.2 H.Q.A.A. Command. I can think of no other reason for my promotion. It just shows how wrong I was about mess nights. I was still not a good soldier.

General Sir Frederick Pile – Tim, as he was known to all concerned – commanded Britain's A.A. Defence from the beginning until the end of the war. He was the only general to remain unmoved either mentally or physically through the whole operation. He was a great personality and a man of remarkable foresight. He was what might be termed a political general who did not hesitate to bypass the normal channels of communication, which made him unpopular with his military colleagues. He was a good picker of men and equally ruthless in removing them if they failed him. He had a generous touch of the 'blarney'. He was, in my opinion, a great commander and I do not believe that any man could have done the job either as well or for so long. Naturally he had enemies but he also had friends and not only in high places.

One of the most difficult tasks of A.A. Command was to maintain good relationships with the R.A.F. and particularly Fighter Command which was situated in the house next door at Stanmore. Although we were honorary members of each other's messes R.A.F. officers seldom came to ours, which was understandable

as it was in the golf club a mile away. Very few of us ever went
to Fighter Command, although their mess was only a hundred
yards from our offices. This was a pity. The only occasion when I
was aware of any disagreeable communication was on the morning of D-Day when Tim Pile, Whitaker, the Brigadier General
Staff, the G.S.O.1 and I went across to the Fighter Command
operations room to see what was going on. A tough R.A.F. ser-
geant refused us admittance and despite the glittering display of
brass he was adamant that nobody, but nobody, was to be allowed
to pass. So there was nothing to be done about it but to retire. What
was said on the telephone later I don't know. I went off to breakfast.

One morning I was sent for by the M.G.G.S. and told that I
would be going to the Staff College on one of the war courses.
This was as big a shock to me as it subsequently proved to them.
It was nevertheless an honour which was ill-deserved. Of all my
experiences both before and since I can truthfully say that I have
never been through such a thorough and efficient period of mental
training. By that time the Army had learned its lesson, very often
the hard way, and the result was most impressive. The Commandant was Douglas Wimberley and the Deputy Commandant Julian
Gascoigne, both men of great ability, distinction and experience.
Consequently the staff under them were of a very high order. A
great percentage of those on the course had had battle experience
in some theatre of the war. Those who were regulars and who
survived the final months of the campaign and many of the students in the same category achieved the rank of brigadier or above.

I just managed to pass the course but only by the skin of my
teeth. I was treated as a fully fledged 'gunner', which, by the
greatest stretch of imagination I certainly was not. My answers to
questions were, to say the least of it, definitely 'off target'. This
introduced a certain touch of originality into our syndicate discussions. Had some of my solutions been adopted in real warfare many
men would have died at the hands of our own artillery. My only
consolation, if such a term can be used, is that similar experiences
have occurred in Vietnam.

It was at the Staff College, where I was installed in the pleasant
surroundings of Minley Manor, that I met Gilbert Nixon. I formed
a close friendship with him. He was militarily everything that I
was not. He was a star pupil. He had fought in the desert and had

been awarded the M.C. He was a great help to me as I struggled through papers which posed questions I could not understand, let alone answer. Without his assistance I am sure that I would have failed the course.

After the war he became Commanding Officer of the Liverpool Scottish when the Territorial Army was reconstituted. One day he came to see me at the House of Commons where I often entertained him when he came to London. I was then Secretary of the Conservative Party's Army Sub-Committee. He told me that he was not to be granted an extension of his command which was the normal practice when the C.O. had performed his duties efficiently. This astonished me when he told me that no good reason had been given for this decision. That again was unusual not to say irregular. Knowing Gilbert, I suspected he might have fallen out with his brigadier. I promised to help and I wrote at once to Jim Hutchison, the Under-Secretary at the War Office, who had a distinguished war record and who was a friend of mine. He was very cagey and said that the matter was settled and could not be reopened. I was even more amazed, and not a little annoyed, when it transpired that Gilbert's successor was to be a Regular soldier with no associations with the Liverpool Scottish. I took the matter up again, complaining that this was an extraordinary decision. If no Territorial officer was available it seemed crazy to refuse a Territorial C.O. an extension of command, especially when recruitment for the T.A. was so poor. But Jim and the War Office were adamant.

Then one evening when I was in the smoking room at the House I opened the evening paper to see Gilbert's picture staring out at me under the headline 'The Colonel Dies of Shame'. He had been involved in homosexual gatherings in Somerset and at Taunton Assizes had been sentenced to a term of imprisonment. In the cells he had taken poison – a cyanide capsule, I think – and died. He was a chemist and had access to such things. He had been married a year before and had a little girl. I had met his wife who was a very sweet person.

Although I can normally detect homosexual tendencies of the active kind in people and although I had known Gilbert extremely well since 1944 I never suspected him of this and he never acted in any way or made any remark which would have pointed to it. This was a great shock to me and a great lesson in human psychology. Here was a man who had fought with great courage and who was prepared to take his own life in the face of a fate which, I assume, he must have considered worse than death. And there is no humour in that remark. Apparently he had previously been apprehended for soliciting in Liverpool which accounted for the decision not to extend his command. This the Army knew. Gilbert never admitted this to me. Had we known each other better I think he would have done so.

When I had completed my Camberley course in December 1944 I was sent for by the War Office and, after an interview with a rather tired brigadier, I was told that it was considered that it would be a good thing if I went on a further course to learn Japanese so that when the war in the Far East was over I could help to clean up the mess there. At that point the real mess had not occurred. I was not exactly thrilled by this prospect as, among other reasons, I knew that Japanese was a very difficult language to learn. I then reminded the Brigadier that I was an adopted prospective Conservative candidate and that when the war in Europe was over my services would be required in the Don Valley. This distressed the War Office not a little as they had omitted to do their 's.d.' as homework was called at the Staff College. I spent a month unemployed, which suited me, as it was over Christmas. I was then appointed Brigade Major of 100 A.A. Brigade in the Second Army which then had its headquarters at Weert in Holland. I was delighted by this appointment, as my old regiment was in the Brigade and it meant meeting old friends again. There was another reason for my pleasure. The anti-aircraft units of Second Army were under the control of a brigadier who disliked A.A. Command so much that when the forces for Europe were assembled he refused to have anyone around him who he regarded as a 'Tim Pile' man. There was no more fervent 'Tim Pile' man than myself. I had never met him but what I had heard about him I did not like. I only met him once after my appointment and that was once too often. He was one of those men who believed that it was necessary to be rude to be effective; unfortunately war produces too many of these in high places.

Also in 100 A.A. Brigade was 107 H.A.A. Regiment which was the A.A. Regiment of the H.A.C. It contained Major E. R. G. Heath whom I had known at Oxford in the Union and in the O.U. Conservative Association. I think it worth recording that when I was sitting on the banks of the Elbe with his Commanding Officer Colonel Slater after the war was over we were discussing politics. He said, 'I think Teddy will one day be Prime Minister.' So many people are now claiming that they made similar predictions that I feel I must give credit where credit is truthfully due. I remember that I replied, 'In politics almost anything can happen,' and left him to work that one out.

We temporary soldiers found during the war that those Regulars who were good were very, very good and those who were bad were horrid. My two Brigade Commanders in Germany were betwixt and between: one was hidebound and the other was stupid. Both had a nasty feeling that the war would end before they became generals. Fortunately for everyone, except the Germans, it did. They both disliked me, particularly because I had been at the Staff College and they had not. The former was a stickler for security. We were forbidden when we were in Holland to suggest that the next objective was the Maas. When we had crossed that without much difficulty it was similarly forbidden to speak about the Rhine. After that he left us. Had he been in the highest position of command I suspect we could easily have gone back over the Seine by mistake.

My second brigadier was a nice man but only capable of one thought an hour, which tended to hold things up. One evening when we had been to a conference and it was essential that we get the orders out as quickly as possible he insisted on taking me for a walk to listen to the birds in order to clear his mind. Whilst he listened to the birds I endeavoured to get the orders into my mind.

In the last four months of the war the Brigade saw little action as our target, the Luftwaffe, no longer operated effectively. During the crossing of the Rhine it was suspected that the Germans, having few aircraft, would endeavour to blow up the bridges with mines floated down the river. We were assigned the task of preventing this and for the purpose were allotted a troop of anti-tank gunners and a naval detachment with an Asdic. The sailors were a very jolly lot who treated the whole thing as a joke and spent most of the time drinking and playing gramophone records. The Brigadier apparently did not speak to sailors, so he never visited them, which was just as well.

The day after this equipage was established they triumphantly

reported that they had destroyed eighty mines. This caused great
excitement and I went down to see for myself. I must frankly admit
that I thought that I saw at least a dozen mines blown up. The score
was well over one hundred and fifty when the proceedings had to
be brought to a halt as our troops were all on the other side and
ricochets were landing on them. There were congratulations all
round as the bridge was still intact. Oddly enough it remained
so, although there was nothing to stop any further mines hitting
it. In due course the C.O. received the O.B.E. for his part in the
action. After the war German records proved that there were no
mines available to float down the river. He retained the O.B.E.,
although Britain did not retain the Empire. But it was a nice re-
minder of past glories.

When we ourselves crossed the Rhine we took up our residence
in a very pleasant Schloss near Xanten. This had been desecrated
by our paratroopers, although there was no sign that they had been
resisted except by some swans, one of which had been shot. The
Brigadier demanded that I should have the place cleaned up by
sending for troops from the regiments. I pointed out, as always
'with respect' which was the accepted way of prefacing a strong
objection, that the regiments were under strength. For some reason which I never fathomed there were some Italian prisoners of
war available. The Brigadier protested that he detested 'wops',
so I made the R.S.M. promise to keep them out of sight.

The Brigadier always insisted on having his own portable lava-
tory with him wherever he went and this had been set up at an
appropriate distance from his caravan. One bright morning when
I was going through the mail with him, which was a tedious and
lengthy business at the best of times, he suddenly rose and announced that the cold had got at his bladder. A few minutes later
there was a noise like a bomb exploding which brought the R.S.M.
and his staff running from the orderly room. I remained calm and
wondered what sort of a man my third brigadier would be. But
no such luck. On arrival at his destination the Brigadier had found
a 'wop' seated upon his sacred shrine. It was as if someone had
thrown an egg at the high altar in St. Peter's. Orders were given for
the immediate removal of all 'wops' from the premises. This order
I countermanded once the Brigadier had set off on his morning
visit to the troops.

The other dramatic experience which occurred with the Brigadier was not at all funny. A message was received from VIII Corps instructing us to send a regiment to Belsen as activity on the Rhine had now ceased. On looking at the map I noted that Belsen was far beyond the enemy lines, but Corps assured me that things were now moving so fast that this was no longer the case as the Third Reich was now hurtling to its destruction somewhat in advance of the predicted thousand years which had started in 1933. It was agreed that 113 L.A.A. Regiment should go. This was a wise choice as things turned out as it had originally been the Durham Light Infantry and was commanded by a tough Yorkshireman with both feet on the ground. Neither I, nor they, nor Corps knew the purpose of their journey; if Corps did they omitted to tell me. I saw them off in the very early hours on a journey of about two hundred miles. Their padre, incidentally, was a Jew by birth. For him it must have been a particularly terrible ordeal.

The next day the Brigadier decided to go for a 'swan' to see what went on at Belsen. That evening as I was sitting in the mess a very ashen-faced man came back. It was I think a great tribute to the Army's medical precautions that, so far as I know, no man was taken seriously ill. A few weeks later a party of M.P.s paid a visit to Belsen as the war was over. One of them contracted a virus illness from which he never recovered. The woman of the party was so mentally distressed that she subsequently committed suicide.

Shortly after this we moved up to Luneburg in preparation for crossing the Elbe on our way to Hamburg. But before we could do this Germany surrendered. I stood at the gate of the house we occupied watching a German armoured division driving back through our lines to captivity. On the faces of the men were a strange mixture of expressions; some were downcast, some were obviously relieved and some were just blank.

I returned to England where, owing to the appointment of General Freyberg as Governor General of New Zealand, the constituency of Spelthorne in Middlesex where he had been selected as prospective Conservative candidate had to find a replacement. They asked me to take it on and with reluctance I obtained my release from my friends in Don Valley. I now prepared to enter Parliament. But I and the Conservative Party were in for a nasty shock.

2 Tory Glory Hallelujah

The captains of Toryism in the past can be made the instructors of Toryism in the present: and the Tory tradition is the Tory hope.

GEOFFREY BUTLER

WHEN I went up to Oxford I knew nothing about party politics. I think I had always been a Conservative in spirit. I actually made the decision to join the Party after considering two possible courses of action: both were based upon conceit. At nineteen one is entitled to be conceited.

After six weeks at the Union I came to regard the Conservatives as lazy and uninspiring with a strong touch of snobbery. It was admittedly a pretty swift judgement, but it was not all that inaccurate. The Socialists were intellectually arrogant and self-righteous and were, in the main, extremely dreary people. The Liberals were largely do-gooders. To my mind the Conservatives were too far to the right and the Socialists too far to the left. Even at that time I thought the Liberals belonged to a party of no importance. In that I was a little ahead of Michael Foot who might have converted me to the Liberal cause had he tried.

I had therefore to decide on my mission, for mission it had to be as I was not interested in side-line politics. Either I would join the Conservatives and try to push them to the left or I would join the Socialists and try to pull them to the right. It was pretty ambitious stuff. Having surveyed the red ties and glowering faces on the Union benches I opted for the Conservatives. They were at that time very much the minority party. This was a situation I decided to change and I take full credit for having done so. Christo-

pher Hollis, in his history of the Oxford Union, referred to me
in not entirely complimentary terms as a kind of political organiser
whose activities made people bored with politics. I gladly accept
the first description but facts do not sustain the second. He was
not, after all, of my generation and was not around to see what
went on.

Within a year the Oxford University Conservative Association
was built up from less than six hundred members to well over
fifteen hundred. George Hutchison has since given the credit
for this to Edward Heath, but this is a tribute I cannot accept, although Heath was as well aware of the importance of political
organisation then as he is today. In fact that is the secret of his
success. But on this particular occasion the work had been done
for him. The strength of this organisation was a great help when it
came to elections at the Union where the Conservatives soon became the majority element. It was also to be significant in the
contests which were to take place in the future over the representation of the University in the House of Commons.

In due course I became Secretary and then Librarian of the
Union and ultimately contested the Presidency against my friend
Bill Shebbeare whom I defeated. During my Presidency an attempt
was made to allow women to become members of the Union. I
was resolutely opposed to this because I found them tedious and
emotional as speakers, and I also felt that they would get themselves elected to office on their looks rather than on their apti-
tude. A vote of all the members was taken. The elderly clergymen,
who were life members and who lived in Oxford, marched behind
me to a man. The Conservatives backed me because they had got
into the habit of doing so and because I had warned them that
nearly all garrulous women were Socialists. The proposal was defeated. The organisation man had won. Today women are members and the Union is facing bankruptcy; so far women Presidents
have shown no signs of being in the same political class as many of
their male predecessors. Another of my actions as President was
to present the Press with a new press bench, as the old one was
extremely narrow and inadequate. It was officially inaugurated by
the editor of the *Oxford Mail*. I had already appreciated the importance of good press relations for a politician. I also stopped
a move by the Socialists to abolish the wearing of evening dress
by the officers and main speakers: I told the elderly clergymen

that they were intending to turn up in bathing dresses and I really
think they believed me. I was also learning how to make use of
a proper relationship between the Church and State which I suppose made me a 'high Tory', but that I would never admit.

As I have said, the senior Conservatives in the University, unlike their Socialist counterparts, G. D. H. Cole, Patrick Gordon-
Walker and Dick Crossman, did nothing at all to assist the
undergraduates. Consequently when they selected the President of
Hertford, an unprepossessing individual called Crutwell, as the
Conservative candidate for the 'burgesship' made vacant by the
retirement of Lord Hugh Cecil, we decided to revolt. Admittedly
we had no vote but we were potential voters and we felt we had
the right to be consulted. We decided that the man for us was
Professor Lindemann, better known as 'Prof'. Lindemann had
made a great reputation for himself in the first war by declaring
that he knew how to get an aircraft out of a spin-dive. When people
refused to believe him he took one up, put it into a spin-dive, and
proved his point.

Although 'Prof' had up to that time done little more than anyone else in the senior common rooms to assist us, we felt that this
was a man with a contribution to make to affairs. What was more
he was a fighter and we were in fighting mood having been told
by the senior Conservatives, known as 'the caucus', to mind our
own business. 'Prof' was a great hater as well, which meant that
he had more enemies than friends. This was not exactly an asset
in a parliamentary candidate, as was indeed proved.

One of his closest friends was Winston Churchill, who was
then in the wilderness. We decided, despite the fact that 'Prof'
was not a good public speaker, to hold a pre-election meeting with
Winston as guest. This, to my knowledge, had never been done in
university politics before, so it had the added attraction of annoy-
ing the Crutwellians. It also annoyed Conservative Central Office
whom we irreverently regarded as a collection of incompetent
'fuddy-duddies'. The chief attraction was, of course, Churchill.
I was summoned to attend at 'Prof's' rooms before the meeting in
order to put the great man in the picture. I was planted in a chair
on one side of the fireplace with Churchill on the other. He was
smoking a cigar and drinking Scotch; I was given a glass of sherry
and a box of chocolate peppermint creams – rather a strange mixture. It was an alarming but exciting experience. Churchill never

spoke to me again when I became a member of Parliament except to thank me for putting up the maps at the meeting when he explained the Suez policy to the Conservative Parliamentary Defence Committee. Even then he mistook me for a House of Commons servant which, in a sense, I was. 'Prof' lost the election despite the fact that the meeting was a great success: unfortunately few of those present had votes.

'Prof' had a splendid manservant, a veritable Jeeves, who also had the distinction of being named Harvey. Consequently I often received strange communications addressed to Harvey from people and organisations with whom Lindemann did not wish to make personal contact. Harvey was a great snob as befitted a man in his position. One day when I was talking to him in Christ Church Meadow I noticed that 'Prof's' dog, which he was exercising, had made contact with another dog which was something which was never allowed. When I pointed this out Harvey replied, 'That is quite all right, sir. That is Lord Birkenhead's dog.'

One night during the war, when I was visiting Christ Church, I sat next to 'Prof' at High Table. He was in great spirits as he had just prevented the Warden of Wadham, a man called Stenning, from getting an extension to his term of office. Recounting this to me, he observed, 'But he's got his own back, he's become an air-raid warden.' I laughed but I noticed that no one else did. I also laughed when 'Prof' became Lord Cherwell which infuriated his colleagues some of whom were only just prevented from throwing themselves into it.

My support of the Lindemann candidature did not endear me to Conservative Central Office and my popularity further decreased when a Conservative M.P., sent by them to address the University Association, ended his meeting amidst cat-calls and jeers despite the fact that only Conservatives were present. He made such a ludicrous speech that when question time arrived he was asked whether it was Conservative colonial policy to flog all natives with bicycle chains. This he took seriously and was greatly incensed. He then declared that he had lost his train of thought, which was asking for trouble, and there was an outburst of railway noises. He left the meeting shouting, 'You're a lot of Socialist swine.' I subsequently received a furious letter from Miss Marjorie Maxse, whom I subsequently grew to admire greatly, saying that if there were any more meetings like that there would be no more speakers.

I tartly replied that if there were any more speakers like that there would be no more meetings. My name was no doubt moved up several places on the Conservative black list. But much worse was to come.

When I came down I decided that I would become a prospective Conservative candidate for Parliament. I went to see Lord Windlesham, who was unkindly known to my generation of Conservatives as Lord Swindle-'em. There was some reason for this, although it was not altogether his fault. In fact in those days the Chairman of the Party was little more than a figurehead crushed between the Leader and the formidable General Director, Sir Robert Topping, and overshadowed by the personality of Miss Marjorie Maxse.

Lord Windlesham explained to me that there were three classes of Conservative seat for Parliament. Class 1 were safe. In this class the candidate was expected to make a substantial financial contribution in the region of a thousand pounds a year, pay the agent's salary, contribute to local charities and join all the appropriate local clubs. This amounted to about three thousand pounds a year. Class 2 seats were normally held by the Party, but as there was a danger of losing them the contribution was reduced according to the risk, but it was normal to pay over one's parliamentary salary. Class 3 seats were hopeless and the reward was the honour of fighting for the Party. Here again it was likely that the election expenses would have to be found but little else, and in certain circumstances a grateful party might fork out a small sum. I had always known that this disgraceful state of affairs existed, but I had never thought that it was condoned with such equanimity and even approval by the hierarchy. But with all that brandy behind one what was three thousand pounds? Windlesham was, of course, a Hennessy. It is gratifying to note that his present successor has a more progressive view of affairs. If he did not he would not be one of Edward Heath's Ministers.

I soon found on my excursions in search of a seat that everything Lord Windlesham had said was true. Scarborough was the most expensive and they also demanded that I should live in the constituency in an appropriate house. Nevertheless, I liked Yorkshire and I was soon adopted for the Don Valley. Here there was a Labour majority of 19,999 and Tom Williams, the sitting member, was a charming and moderate man who was extremely popular with everyone and with good reason. He was to become a first-class Minister of Agriculture. I told my new Association that I felt our objective must be to stop his majority getting to 20,000. Being essentially practical people, they accepted this as a reasonable target.

At this point in my political career I decided to strike at the system of selecting candidates, so I set down in a memorandum all that Lord Windlesham had told me and much else besides. Before circulating it to all M.P.s and candidates I gave a copy to a friend, who was then working on the *Evening Standard*. To my surprise they featured it as a front-page story. It appeared on the evening before a meeting of the Conservative Universities Associations. There was a reception to which I went and was received somewhat coolly by Lord Windlesham: there was no double brandy for me that night. But Miss Maxse gave me a wink and I have a feeling she agreed with me as she believed in merit as opposed to wealth. Many years later the Maxwell-Fyfe Committee endorsed all that I had written but by that time the old men of reaction were on their way out.

As prospective candidate for Don Valley I had to decide whether I supported Chamberlain over Munich. Despite his unfortunate speech on his return from that ignominious settlement I do not believe he was really under any illusions as to Hitler's ultimate intentions. I was in fact present at a private dinner party at the Carlton Club the year before it happened when he said that the object of British foreign policy must be to drive the Germans against the Russians. But Ribbentrop and Molotov knew better. In 1938 Chamberlain realised that Britain was not equipped to go to war and it was also clear that the French were not prepared to go to war. For this state of affairs the responsibility rested on the shoulders of Baldwin; nor were the Labour leaders completely blameless. When he was in government Herbert Morrison had expressed his opposition to all forms of military training in schools. Just as the Conservatives were hampered in their anti-Nazi activities by their fear of Communism so the Socialists were handicapped by their pacifism.

I believed, in the circumstances, that Chamberlain had no alternative at Munich. This was not the view of many of the younger Conservatives and when a by-election occurred at Oxford they joined in supporting A. D. Lindsay, the Master of Balliol, who stood as an all-party candidate against Quintin Hogg and coined the slogan 'A vote for Hogg is a vote for Hitler'. Amongst those who joined that cause was Edward Heath. Despite this handicap Quintin won.

One of the more foolish accusations made by the left wing which arose at that time was that the Conservative Party had Fascist leanings. Both Hitler and Mussolini were far more Socialist than they were Conservative and the Nazi Party was, as its name indicates, a National Socialist Party. The titles Labour and Conservative are misleading and left and right are descriptions which can be equally inaccurate.

One of the elements in the Conservative Party which was regarded as secretly pro-German and reactionary was the so-called 'Cliveden set' after the name of Lady Astor's house in Buckingham. Consequently I was somewhat surprised to receive a telegram inviting me to stay the weekend there. I assumed that it was a practical joke and rang up to make certain. I was informed that it was not a joke and that I was expected. So I went. It was all very grand. I had never been to a house of that kind before and I have been to few since. Joseph Kennedy and most of his family were there. I can't say that I liked him. The conversation was of a very general nature and my most vivid recollection was having the most marvellous hot chocolate for tea. On the Sunday evening we went to hear carols at Eton where one of the Kennedy boys was at school. I suppose it must have been Edward.

During 1939 I continued my activities in Don Valley although the storm clouds were clearly gathering. I made a point of going down all the pits in the constituency which convinced me that nationalisation was probably the best thing for their future. I did not go so far as to say so in public although I expressed the view to my chairman who was horrified. On one occasion I went down a pit in the morning prior to addressing the Rotarians in Doncaster. I forgot to put grease under my eyes so that when I had my shower afterwards I could not get the coal dust out. Consequently I had to go to the lunch looking as though I had been in a fight. After the meeting one of the Rotarians observed to my chairman, 'Scruffy-looking bugger, your candidate.' After my remarks on nationalisation I think he probably agreed.

With the war my political activities ended. I was at one point interviewed by the Windsor Conservative Association whose

Treasurer was a friend of mine. They asked me if I would be prepared to resign from the Army if I was elected to Parliament, as an M.P. was entitled to do. I said I was not. Even if I had been prepared to do this I doubt if I should have been selected. In any case, despite my undistinguished war record, it would have been on my conscience for the rest of my life. There were others of my age who had no such inhibitions. I am sorry for them.

As I have mentioned, when the war ended I was invited by the Spelthorne Constituency in Middlesex to contest the General Election of 1945. It had been a safe seat but had been readjusted by the Boundaries Commission which, from time to time, throws its shadow across the path of Members of Parliament who had thought themselves installed for life. Nevertheless, at the time of my selection neither I nor the Spelthorne Conservative Association, which was practically non-existent, were really worried. But that did not last long. We soon found that there was a spirit abroad which was decidedly anti-Conservative.

Assuming that the country's gratitude to Churchill would ensure them victory, the Conservative Party went into battle practically unprepared. In justice to them it must be accepted that many of their candidates and agents and members of the local Associations had been away on war service. This was also true of the Labour Party but not to the same extent. This fact led to a good deal of bitterness after the election was over.

The final blow to Conservative hopes came when the Forces' votes were counted. It was clear that the other ranks in all the services were predominantly pro-Labour. They regarded the Conservatives as the party of the officer class, just as the workers still regarded them as the party of the bosses. It is difficult to argue that they were wrong at that stage. Many candidates, including myself, made the mistake of using photographs of ourselves in uniform for our election addresses and of using our military titles. Although the campaign was fought on the programme of food, work and homes, the posters and literature were largely covered with pictures of Churchill.

Churchill and his colleagues were out. He refused the Order of the Garter on the grounds that he had already been given the order of the boot. At least he retained his sense of humour. But he was very sore, as indeed we all were. Although not surprising in view of what was to happen, it was not particularly wise for the Socialists to cry 'We are the masters now' and to sing 'The Red Flag' in the corridors of power. Neither, in retrospect, was it surprising that the Conservatives should have been defeated. They had been in power since 1931. Ten years had passed since the last election and there were now many new electors to consider. The Conservatives were blamed, quite reasonably, for the errors which had led to the war and for Britain's lack of preparation. The younger generation wanted a change and were quite ready to give Labour a chance. Many of the older generation were frankly bored with the old faces.

Psychologically the Labour Party had a much clearer idea of the way the tide was flowing than the Conservatives had. They did not make the mistake of assuming that there was such a thing as gratitude in politics. In the interests of democracy it was a good thing that the Labour Party won the General Election of 1945. A party that stays in power too long gets stale and has too little time to think : a party that stays in opposition too long becomes frustrated and irresponsible.

For a period after 1945 the Conservatives were in a dazed condition. It was then that R. A. Butler emerged as the Party's thinker and gathered around him a team of young men who were capable of working out the objectives of the Party in its new role. Prominent members were Iain Macleod, Reginald Maudling, and Enoch Powell. To 'R.A.B.' the Party owes much of its achievements in the 'fifties. To him, above all, it owes the fact that it ceased to be regarded as the stupid party. It would be unfair to those who went before him, and to some of those who have subsequently disagreed with him, to take the line that intelligence in politics is everything. Many intelligent men have made complete political fools of themselves, whilst many who have paid more attention to practicalities than to political thought have succeeded. It is a question of judgement and of balance, the absence of which has destroyed Labour Governments in the postwar period. To them and to all politicians I would offer the advice of Thomas Mann, 'Think as men of action, act as men of thought'.

The Conservative Charters were born under R. A. Butler, whose ultimate failure to become leader of the Conservative Party was due, strangely enough, to lack of both judgement and balance. Churchill took little part in this part of the operation. It was always his view that a party in opposition should not show its hand too clearly in the field of policy. He adhered to the view that people vote against governments and not for them, and there is a great deal of truth in this although not so much now since people are politically better informed due largely to the influence of television. He did, however, take one step which was every bit as important as the work of Butler and his team. He appointed Lord Woolton, the highly successful Minister of Food in the National Government, as Chairman of the Conservative Party. As Woolton himself said, 'It is no good producing goods if you can't sell them.' And no one knew better how to sell goods than he did. So Butler produced the goods, Woolton sold them and Churchill reaped the reward.

The strength of the Conservative Party lies in its adaptability which amounts to intelligent and responsible pragmatism. Its weakness lies in a tendency not to think far enough ahead on the grounds that this does not amount to practical politics. The Charters did much to remedy this fault. These were criticised by their opponents within the Party because they committed them to various courses of action which were not, in their opinion, in keeping with previous Conservative thought. But under Baldwin and Chamberlain there had not been enough thought and during the war there were other things to think about.

During the 'fifties the gap between the parties narrowed and this was a danger to both of them. To a considerable extent the Conservatives adapted the better aspects of Socialism. Their refusal to de-nationalise the already nationalised industries was sensible, although it was resented by the right wing of the Party and by a number of industrialists. Such a process which would have involved re-nationalisation by any future Labour Government would have led to industrial and commercial chaos. The risk they ran as a result of this and as a result of the progressive policies of Harold Macmillan was that they would be regarded by the uncommitted voter as a Socialist Party in disguise and people would argue that it would be better to have real Socialism rather than semi-Socialism.

The Socialists too were in danger of losing their identity and they were under continuous pressure from the left wing of the Party to move further to the left. But the experience of the 1945–50 Labour Government had taught the leadership that it is dangerous to go too far too fast. They had come to realise that the

British people are instinctively conservative in their reaction. Those who attack institutions are liable to destroy themselves and not the institutions. To a considerable extent the result of the General Election of 1970 reflected this. The next few years will show where the party system is going: at the present time it would be difficult to predict.

Meanwhile back in 1945 the young hopefuls of the Party like myself were out in search of seats to contest. When I returned to Mather and Crowther on the morning after my defeat my old friend and boss, Gordon Boggon, said cheerfully, 'Don't worry, I'll soon find you a seat.' This struck me as a somewhat illogical statement even from him. He then explained that he was a great friend of Aneurin Bevan, which was true. The fact that I was not a Socialist seemed to him secondary in importance to my becoming an M.P. He was essentially a representative of the old school of advertising.

Needless to say, I did not take up his offer, although I was to become a great personal admirer of Aneurin Bevan in the years to come. It is I believe one of the strengths of the House of Commons that men can oppose each other on the floor of the House, often with great bitterness, and then drink together in the smoking room. Those who find this impossible often prove to be the least effective politicians. Personal antagonisms are bad for the political digestion and can also be bad for political reputations.

Spelthorne naturally blamed me for losing the election although I doubt if General Freyberg would have done much better. So I was out there. Owing to the heavy defeats at the election there was little point in trying for a by-election as there were a number of distinguished people that the Party wanted back in the House of Commons.

I was a member of the Carlton Club and of the Junior Club in those days. Some people think that they are connected but this is not so. All that their members share is an obligation to declare allegiance to the principles of the Conservative Party. It has been unkindly said that the Carlton Club is for those who have got on in politics and the Junior Carlton is for those who are still trying. That also is not true.

The Carlton Club was once the centre of great influence in the Party when power was wielded by the great and the wealthy, and it was also the centre of political intrigue when politics in high places was conducted in that way. With the changed character of the Party and of society all that has mercifully become a thing of the past. Even after the war it still had its place and many Conservative M.P.s were members. During the war the old club in Pall Mall was bombed and it moved to Arthur's, a club which it had taken over just before hostilities. The premises were not nearly so grand but they were more homely and less expensive to run. The members of Arthur's mingled unobtrusively with the members of the Carlton Club and I suspect that the two old men whom I overheard having the following conversation were in fact members of the old Arthur's club.

The one said to the other, 'I have just read a book by a man called Havelock Ellis.'

'Havelock Wilson, that's the Palestine fellah, isn't it?'

'No, no, Havelock Ellis!'

'Never heard of him.'

'Neither had I. But in this book he says that ten per cent of the male population of this country are sexual perverts.'

'That's not a very nice thing to say, is it.'

'No, and it's even less nice when you think that there are nearly a thousand members of this club.'

For obvious reasons I found this interchange extremely amusing, although, looking around me, I could not help feeling that Havelock Ellis must have made a mistake in his calculations. But then he was never a member of the Carlton Club.

It is not, therefore, surprising that the influence of the Carlton Club has waned. In order to encourage new members they have installed a one-armed bandit in the bar. In the old days two Cabinet Ministers would have done the trick.

The Junior Carlton Club was full of active members of the Party and did more to promote its interests in London and it still does. Although I did not seek the office I became Chairman of the Political Committee as a result of a palace revolution against the existing Chairman who had been in office a long time and was considered by the younger members to be a crashing bore. He never believed that I had had nothing to do with his removal and, as he knew me well, I can understand that. A grateful party has now given him a knighthood. So we must all have been mistaken—or were we?

It was my task in this exalted position to plan the programme of speakers for the year and to submit it to the Committee for their approval. Leslie Hore-Belisha had just come over to the Party from the National Liberals. He was an old friend of mine and was also an ex-President of the Oxford Union. Offensive people said that his real name was Horeb Elisha and that he had changed it by deed-poll. In actual fact his name was originally Leslie Belisha and he added the name Hore as a tribute to his stepfather, Sir Adair Hore, who had always been good to him.

When I submitted my list one member of the Committee objected to the inclusion of Hore-Belisha's name. In this he received support from other members. I pointed out that this was a man who had been a Cabinet Minister and had seen fit to join our party and that I thought it appropriate that we should indicate our appreciation. We were, after all, out of power and it was much more fashionable for people to join the Socialist band wagon. But the opposition continued. So I then said that I was willing to withdraw Hore-Belisha's name if the Committee would agree to my approaching the Chairman on their behalf with the request that the statue of Disraeli be removed from the premises. There was instant denial that their gesture was in any way anti-semitic and I was assured that it was due only to the fear that no one would come to hear Hore-Belisha's speech. To this ridiculous suggestion I retorted that if no one did I would resign. My proposal was then accepted and on the night the meeting was packed. He gave a great performance.

Meanwhile I continued my search for a seat and finally I arrived before the selection committee of the Harrow East Conservative Association. It was a seat which had been created by the Boundaries Commission and had been carved out of the two larger constituencies of Harrow and Hendon which had expanded to unwieldy proportions. In 1945 it had been won by the Labour Party for many of the same reasons as Spelthorne. As at Spelthorne it had been decided to select a new candidate although the former candidate wanted to continue. His name was Ashe Lincoln and he had upset a number of people by his pro-Zionist activities. He was, therefore, still in the running but his chances of selection were not good.

Apart from myself there were two other contestants, John Vaughan-Morgan and Ronald Bell, both of whom were to become M.P.s for safe seats. In this connection I record a wise piece of advice given to me by my old friend John Carvel, the Lobby Correspondent of *The Star*, whose career in political journalism was damaged by the leak over Hugh Dalton's Budget which resulted in the Chancellor's resignation. It was John Carvel, who lived at Pinner just outside the Harrow East boundary, who suggested I put my name forward for the seat. He told me to fight a seat which was held by Labour rather than to try for a safe seat.

Apart from the credit it would give me in the eyes of the Party it was an established fact that very few young men who had been elected for safe seats since the war had made their mark in Parliament. This has certainly proved true in the case of Edward Heath, Enoch Powell, and a number of others, although Maudling and Macleod never had to fight for their political lives. But they had the advantage of being Butler boys.

I prepared a splendid little speech for the Harrow East selection committee outlining my views on party philosophy and policy. This was received politely but with no great enthusiasm. When it came to questions the Chairman asked me, 'Do you drink?', to which I replied, 'Naturally, I am a Scotsman.' This was wildly applauded. I had won the selection.

Lest it should be thought that all Conservative candidates are selected on this basis, or that this was the actual reason for my selection, I think it appropriate to consider the procedure which now exists, especially in the light of my own early attacks on it. What was then regarded as the antics of a rebel are now accepted as orthodox views. Such has been the experience of many rebels in their time. They themseves are then in danger of becoming reactionaries.

There are normally two sources from which candidates are drawn: the local list and the Central Office list. The number of available candidates varies according to the nature of the seat, which is generally safe, marginal or hopeless. In safe seats the local boy, who is often the Chairman, is ambitious to make good because there is little risk of failure. He also runs the risk of making enemies with the Assiciation: politics provides ample opportunity for personal hostilities. Furthermore there is plenty of scope for local jealousy especially amongst the wives. Again the state of the Party at the time has a marked bearing on selection. When a party is in power its 'top brass' is in the House of Commons, when it is out there is a collection of defeated ex-Ministers from which to choose. This also presents a problem both for the ex-Minister and for the selection committee. Should he choose another seat or should he try to restore the lost faith of the electorate in him? If an ex-Minister wants another seat what went wrong in his last one? This is a situation which applies particularly to by-elections when it may be extremely valuable for a depleted party to have one of its exiled hierarchy back. This was very true after 1945.

What is of great importance to the effectiveness of the democratic system is that upon the final selection the ultimate representation of the constituency depends, assuming that the seat is safe or winnable. It is on this issue that the party system is challenged. The contention is that the representation of the great majority depends on the decision of very few people who may be relatively unqualified for partisan or even inexplicable reasons. There is strength in this argument, but even greater strength in the argument that there is no effective alternative. It does therefore place a heavy responsibility on the local constituency association to see that it is democratically organised and that candidate selection is made with the interests of the whole constituency in mind. A Member of Parliament who does not pay full attention to the requirements of all his constituents, whatever their political allegiance, is neglecting his prime duty and is weakening the democratic case.

The strength of the Conservative Party organisation has always rested with women. It is surprising that over the years so few women have been selected as candidates. There have been notable exceptions such as Nancy Astor, Florence Horsburgh, Pat Hornsby-Smith, Betty Harvie-Anderson, and Margaret Thatcher. The basic reason for this is probably psychological. Women despite demands for equality, do not really want to be led by women whom they regard only as equals and often as inferiors. I admit that this is a prejudiced argument but I am guided by experience and not by psychological theory. I also admit that my judgement may be questioned, perhaps rightly, by those who read this book.

Another force in the Conservative Party is that of the Young Conservatives who once went by the name of the Junior Imperial League. It is significant that they have always been stronger than the Young Socialists, who hardly seem to exist, and the Young Liberals; although the latter seem to be turning into a collection of

political 'hippies' who threaten to become more of an embarrassment than an asset to their cause. In more recent years two
other forces have emerged in the Conservative Party – the 'Bow
Group' on the left and the 'Monday Club' on the right. When I
became prospective Conservative candidate for Harrow East neither
existed.

Before I arrived in the final straight towards the House of Commons I had involved myself in local government affairs. At Party
Conferences I had been struck by the general ignorance on the
subject not only on the part of my colleagues but also on the part
of Members of Parliament. Many considered it a vulgar occupation that belonged to tradesmen, which to a great extent it was
and many people were in it to feather their own nests. The Conservative Party had always taken the view that party politics
should be kept out of local government and consequently Conservatives contested elections either as Independents or as rate-
payers. The Labour Party, largely inspired by Herbert Morrison,
put paid to this theory.

As an organisation man I had little sympathy with this loose
form of activity. In principle the independence of local government from central activity has something to recommend it. But
the development of our society has overtaken this parochial approach and the phrase 'keep local government local' makes no
sense against present requirements. In this spirit I first became a
member of the Council of the Royal Borough of Kensington and
then a representative of South Kensington on the London County
Council.

Neither task was particularly arduous, nor did they inspire me,
but doubtless that was my fault. At County Hall the Conservatives
had been out of power since Herbert Morrison won London for
Labour in 1934. Looking around the Conservative benches this
was not altogether surprising, although on this particular occasion
we very nearly won.

The leader of the Conservative opposition was Henry Brooke
whose speeches were only outclassed in their tediousness by those
of the Leader of the Council, Isaac Hayward, who took his orders
from his old boss across the road at Westminster.

I was a member of the Education Committee to which we elected
Peggy Jay, the wife of Douglas Jay, as Chairman. On her election
she took the opportunity of delivering a lecture on the importance

of equality in education with which I entirely agreed. The emotion of the moment was somewhat spoiled by the presence in the gallery of her two sons who have now achieved considerable distinction themselves, but on this occasion they were wearing their Dragon School blazers – not exactly an egalitarian establishment.

One of the most tedious practices of the L.C.C. was to deliver obituary speeches about almost anyone who had had anything to do with the organisation. Henry Brooke surpassed himself in paying a tribute to the Chief Parks Officer, a Mr. Mawson, who had died. With a precision of language which was a cross between a classical don and a girls' school headmistress he told us: 'It is my custom, as you probably know, to walk in the early mornings on Hampstead Heath. This place has been rarified in beauty by the work of the late Mr. Mawson. Now when I take my walks I shall see Mr. Mawson behind every bush.' Hampstead Heath is a well-known haunt of homosexuals on the prowl, but not, of course, in the early morning. Poor Henry Brooke. It was sad that it should fall to him to lose Hampstead with its large Conservative majority to Labour in 1964.

It was largely due to the attitude of the Conservative opposition on the L.C.C. that comprehensive schools were dragged, quite wrongly, into the party political battle. In many respects they are an expansion of the public-school system and where the conditions are right they ought clearly to be established. The argument is clearly not about the principle but about the method. It is to be hoped that this will ultimately be brought home to the warring factions.

Despite my failure to appreciate the nicer points of local government I found my experience of great assistance in dealing with local government matters when I became an M.P. Today many Conservative M.P.s have taken the trouble to gain similar experience which was not the case in the past. The Conservative political machine in local government is now extremely efficient as the result of recent years have shown. With the plans for local government reform now presented by Redcliffe-Maud and Peter Walker this is extremely important for the future of the Party.

When I became their candidate and throughout the time I was the Member, the Harrow East Conservative Assocoation was run by Sir Frederick Handley-Page of aircraft fame. He was a dominant personality in every sense. In business he was both a genius and an autocrat: I am told that he even made his co-directors clock-in each morning. Politically he was not a progressive Conservative but he respected my views, as I respected his, and we never had an argument. This, I think, was rather a disappointment to him as he loved controversy. He once complained to me that since I had been M.P. life in the Association had become very dull as there were never any rows. After we had both gone, he in one direction and I in another, they made up for it and consequently lost the seat. One of the assets of sitting for a vulnerable seat is that the business of holding on to it absorbs the energies of the party members and there is no time for internecine squabbling which would allow the enemy at the gate to break in. It was the energy and support that Handley-Page gave to me and the organisation which enabled us to win Harrow East and, having won, to hold it.

I admit that there were occasions when his not infrequent public utterances caused me mild embarrassment. At a United Nations Association dinner he once said that it was ridiculous to waste money educating niggers who were much happier left alone up their trees. As the Race Relations Board was not in existence at that time to tell people who should, or should not, make Scots porridge, he was not summoned before them. That would have been an occasion in itself at which I should have liked to be present. I was asked at a public meeting if I endorsed the views of my President, to which I replied that I never commented on remarks made outside the constituency. Like Sir Frederick, I got away with it. I was clearly learning fast and I learned a lot from him.

The sitting member for Harrow East was a worthy ex-schoolmaster called Skinnard. His habit of addressing his constituents as if they were still sitting at their desks did not endear him to them. He had no sense of humour and, disastrously for him, no political sense either. My only encounter with him was at a Communist meeting to which he and the Communist candidate had been invited. There was not a single supporter of mine present as the meeting was not in the constituency. Nor were there any supporters for Skinnard. He was the target for their attack which is an endearing aspect of left-wing politics.

During the course of his extremely boring address he dropped his spectacles on the table in front of him. Whilst he was groping for them there was an outburst of offensive laughter. In a pained

c

voice he said, 'I suffer from myopia, that's very funny isn't it?' There was immediate silence. Afterwards he said to me, 'You see, Harvey, I fear you have no hope against me. Once I told them of my infirmity their sympathies were with me. I am truly in their hearts.' To this I replied rather unkindly, 'I don't want to disillusion you but I think they thought you were suffering from an unmentionable disease and they were shocked that you should mention it. In any case I think it is more important for you to be on their voting slips than in their hearts.' When he discovered that I had been right he burst into tears. I was sorry for him but not for Harrow East. I never spoke to or heard of him again.

At the end of 1949 I got married. This satisfied my supporters in the constituency who thought it was a mistake to have a candidate who was a bachelor and over thirty. Similar objections have been expressed in recent years about Edward Heath but they appear to have done him little harm although providing plenty of material for malicious gossip. I agree none the less that it is an asset for an M.P. to be married, provided it is to the right person. In these days, however, divorce proceedings which have been ruinous in the past count for little or nothing. Such is the new morality.

I had announced my engagement in the summer of the year to Clare Mayhew, the youngest sister of one of my Oxford friends, Christopher Mayhew, who was a Labour M.P. and Parliamentary Under-Secretary to Ernest Bevin at the Foreign Office. This caused a certain amount of political excitement. Considering that she was non-political and hated public appearances my wife did extremely well and I am certain she added the newly-weds vote to my total without losing any support, as a result of broken hearts, from the ladies of Harrow East.

The role of a political wife is difficult and it varies according to the constituency and to the M.P. concerned. I have known the wives of some M.P.s who would be better at the job than their husbands and some M.P.s who, without the support of their wives, would have difficulty in holding on to their seats. In the main the Conservative Party does not favour M.P.s' wives who involve themselves actively in the affairs of the constituency association. Those that do are liable to find themselves in active competition with the forceful ladies on the women's advisory committee.

I was always amused to note the different attitudes of M.P.s' wives to political life. For some it was meat and drink and when their husbands achieved office it was heady wine, and when they failed it was like a dose of arsenic. Others played it coolly, treating it as a secondary activity to their home life, and for those who had neither servants nor nannies this meant that it was often very secondary. Some did not play it at all and this could lead to trouble in the constituency.

An objectionable habit which has developed in the Conservative Party is to ask candidates not only to bring their wives but also to ask them to make speeches and to answer questions before the selection committee. They should be reminded that their task is to select a suitable representative for the constituency and not to employ a circus act.

The most dangerous and tiresome political wife is the one who feels it is her duty to promote her husband's political career by taking part in the political power game. This involves a round of social parties, gossip and intrigue with senior Ministers and their wives. This sort of behaviour is not only undesirable, it is 'old hat', and has no place in a progressive democratic organisation. Particularly fatuous and misguided political wives are those who feel it necessary to boost their husbands' egos by applauding their speeches not only in public, which is required of them, but also in private, which is not. They do an ill-service both to the speaker who begins to believe in his ability and to the audience who has to endure his speech. I always permitted my wife three criticisms after each speech, more would have been tedious, and she was allowed to kick me under the table when she thought I had gone on long enough. Usually I escaped this attack by putting my chairman in between us, but my relationship with him was so good that he was quite capable of doing the same thing.

The Labour Government, which came to power in 1945 with an overwhelming majority and had proclaimed the arrival of a hundred years of Socialism, was rocking after five. Its plans for nationalisation which it was fully entitled to bring in were muddled and inefficient in practice, largely because they tried to tackle too many industries too quickly. As Emanuel Shinwell, always a realist, is reported to have said afterwards, 'We did not really know what we were doing.' That is a true epitaph for the first post-war Labour Government, which, unlike its predecessors, was both in office and in power.

It is possible even as an opponent to have some sympathy with

Attlee and his colleagues. They had been in the wilderness for a long time and they had been forced by the war to co-operate with people with whom they were not in agreement. They sincerely believed that the interests of the British people could best be served by Socialism. They underestimated the very considerable problems which confronted them as a result of the devastation of war. Being hostile to the ideas of the Empire, they were not prepared to calculate the cost of being without it. Their worst psychological mistake was to identify the practice of Socialism with wartime controls in the minds of the people. As the people were sick of wartime controls they soon became sick of Socialism.

It can be argued, and any true Socialist must argue, that they were right in trying to make a clean sweep. But democratic politics do not work that way. There must always be a firm base from which to operate. What appears to be the immediate must often be relegated to the ultimate or it may never take place at all. Only a government which has the power to dictate, to crush opposition and, on occasion, to use force, can apply an uninhibited political programme. Only a government which has complete control over all the sources of production, which include the necessities of life, can interfere with the mechanics of industry with impunity. That is possible for the Soviet Union and to a great extent for the United States, but it is not possible for Britain. The fact is that democratic Socialism must operate from democratic foundations which have their origins in the past. To reject past traditions too violently is to endanger future aspirations.

It was not surprising that even after so short a period as five years the Labour Government should be in trouble. Just as the Conservatives had assumed they were going to win in 1945 so, for a considerable period afterwards, had the Labour Government thought that they were impregnable. But they had failed to realise that the decision of 1945 had been made under conditions in which the actual programmes of the parties hardly entered into the argument. By 1948 all this had changed and people were facing up to the realities of peace. They had given the Labour Party the chance they considered they deserved and they had been right to do so; but now they were rapidly reaching the conclusion that things were not working out. The Forces voters who had returned to civil life were disillusioned and the young generation who had just got the vote were finding Socialism restrictive and uninspiring. It was in this atmosphere that I sallied forth to fight the General Election of 1950.

The Harrow East Parliamentary constituency has many advantages to offer a Member of Parliament. It is near to the House of Commons, is closely knit, and contains a reasonably sized electorate which is a representative cross-section of the community. There is no agriculture, and as Alan Herbert wrote in his election address when he fought and won Oxford University, 'I know nothing about agriculture.' There is no heavy industry and the most pressing problems concern housing, transport and various everyday issues. It is very much a commuter society which has now been absorbed into the Greater London Council.

At the time when I was the prospective candidate I was asked whether I would come to live in the constituency if elected. I said I would gladly consider the matter if they would indicate which ward they thought I should live in. It was not so easy to answer this as there were initially six wards: one was wealthy, two were moderately well-off, one was half-and-half and two were relatively poor. Most of my constituents, in whichever ward they lived, had cars and I knew no one who had not got a television set. At that time I had neither.

After careful consideration it was decided that it would probably be better if I were to live just outside the constituency which would avoid the danger of my striking the wrong social note. It would also avoid such private life as I had left being overlooked and my wife could still have arguments if necessary with the tradesmen without losing their votes. So we moved to my old haunt of Richmond where the conditions were very much the same as those in Harrow. I believe it is a great mistake for a Member of Parliament to live far away from his constituency and under different conditions. This is particularly true of widespread constituencies. To understand people and their problems it is necessary to live amongst them and to share their interests.

I did not have much doubt as to the outcome of the 1950 election in Harrow East, barring accidents, although I constantly reminded myself that I had had similar thoughts in Spelthorne. National issues apart, the successful political campaign depends on organisation and to a lesser extent on an active and acceptable candidate. I had spent a considerable amount of time in the constituency following my adoption helping to strengthen the organisation and ensuring that I was seen everywhere in the area. My main dangers were that the sitting member had been there for five years and that the Liberals had a good candidate in Desmond Banks, who has since played a considerable part in the affairs of the Liberal Party. As I have already recounted, the sitting member was not all that popular but the Liberals were likely to get more of my votes than his.

There has always been considerable controversy over whether a Liberal candidate takes more Conservative than Labour votes and whether, when there is no Liberal candidate, Liberals vote Conservative rather than Labour. I do not think there is any complete answer to this and the position can change according to the election issues. Broadly speaking, in the West Country and in Scotland the Liberals are more radically orientated and will not vote Conservative unless the Conservative candidate shows himself to be progressive. Elsewhere it seems to me to be almost evenly split, although the more the Labour Party pursues policies which are considered restrictive to the individual, the more the Liberal vote is likely to go to the Conservatives. A Conservative Party ruled by the members of the 'Monday Club' would undoubtedly drive the Liberals left and I would not blame them even if it meant jumping out of the frying pan into the fire.

We fought the 1950 Election very much on the streets, although it was February and not the best weather for outdoor campaigning. We won the seat by 1,464 and the myopic Skinnard, who had a majority of 6,770 in 1945, was swept away. The Conservatives only narrowly missed winning the whole election; for the Labour Government the writing was on the wall. In the cold morning light I stood outside my hotel on Harrow Hill. I was an M.P. at last. In fact I was a triple politician, being also a member of the London County Council and the Royal Borough of Kensington as well. I was in danger of heading for infallibility; but it was only a temporary illusion.

3 Back Bench. Front Bench

*I believe that, without party, Parliamentary
government is impossible.*

DISRAELI

THE Conservative 'Class of 1950', to use an Americanism, was
not without distinction. They brought a much needed injection
of life into the Parliamentary Party. Many of the existing members
were tired and ageing and many were inadequate. The latter owed
their position to the strange habit of the Conservative Party of
giving safe seats to mediocre people and leaving their brighter
members to fight marginal ones. While this might have kept the
marginal seats, it also meant that in a heavy defeat such as in
1945, their more able M.P.s were knocked out of the House of
Commons.

Iain Macleod, Reginald Maudling, Enoch Powell, Edward
Heath, Aubrey Jones, Cuthbert Alport, and Harold Watkinson
all arrived in the Chamber on that March day in 1950 and took
their seats on the back benches, on which they were to remain for
a shorter time than most of their predecessors. At that time the
House was sitting in the chamber of the House of Lords as the
chamber of the House of Commons was being rebuilt having
been destroyed by bombing during the war.

There is an atmosphere in the House of Commons which no one
who has never been a member can fully understand. The House
has a remarkable ability to tame even the most violent characters.
It has a constantly changing mood which demands immediate
sensitivity. If this mood is not appreciated even the most able

speaker with the best prepared speech can fail. This happened on occasions even to Churchill and to Bevan. Many M.P.s who have become renowned for their performance both on the public platform and on television have never completely succeeded in the House of Commons, which is more concerned with a sincere contribution than with a performance.

This does not mean that M.P.s from time to time do not carry the House with them, even against the tide. But the demand which it makes upon them to make this possible is inherent in its peculiar character. An M.P. who has once succeeded in boring the House finds that it takes him a long time to regain its interest. There is a time for laughter and a time for seriousness but never a time for deception or dreariness. Those who speak must take care to appreciate this or they will find that they have lost the ear of the House and when they have done that the best thing for them to do is to sit down. For those on the front bench this is unfortunately not always possible.

What is it that impels a man to become a Member of Parliament and, having become one, to remain so? To answer that question in detail would require the writing of a separate book with details drawn from the long history of Parliament. It is not an answer which can properly be given in general terms since it involves the personal psychology of individuals. There are, nevertheless, a number of reasons which apply to the majority of members. The most vital is the existence of politics in the blood and the most responsible is a desire to serve the community. The combination of these two produces the most effective and commendable type of M.P. It is of course essential that, possessing these two ingredients, he should be able to communicate.

There are many M.P.s who possess neither and they seldom reach the heights. If they do they contribute little and are soon forgotten after their departure. Those who could be the most dangerous are those who are driven by personal ambition and the lust for power. One of the sources of strength in a Parliamentary democracy is that they are swiftly detected and frustrated in their path. The most tedious are the ones who are there for social distinction. Those who are nothing more than a Parliamentary nuisance are the publicity hounds who seize on every issue, whether it concerns them or not, in order to get their names and faces in the news or on television. It is unfortunate that both the Press and television companies give them ample scope for their activities. I would hope that this book makes it clear in which category I place myself and that this will be accepted. If not it is my fault for not expressing myself clearly, and in a political animal that is a grievous fault.

In March 1950 the Labour Government was depressed and with reason. The illusions of 1945 had been swept away and Socialism seemed to be discredited for all time. They knew they could not last long with their majority of only six. Aneurin Bevan, Harold Wilson and John Freeman put paid to the exercise over the health charges and the game was up. The Conservatives, on the other hand, were inspired by the realisation that the day was not far off when they could put into practice the ideas which had been expressed in the Charters. This at any rate was true of the 'Class of 1950'. The older generation were more concerned with avenging the ignominy of 1945 and they were inclined to look on their new colleagues as starry-eyed idealists who would soon learn the realities of Parliamentary life. Those who had held on after 1945 and were not on the opposition front bench were inclined to resent the arrival of men who they suspected would soon overtake them. They were right in their suspicions. Time was not on their side.

The 'Class of 1950' had an advantage in starting off in opposition. Although it is often said that the Conservatives are not good in opposition this has not been borne out by the facts. The new arrivals showed themselves to be extremely effective, especially the Butler boys, who had the facts at their fingertips. It was at this time that a number of the new back-benchers formed themselves into a group and produced the document entitled 'One Nation'. The leader of the group, in so far as there was a leader, was Iain Macleod, who quickly established himself as the brightest star in the new firmament. Others included Edward Heath, Robert Carr, Cuthbert Alport and Enoch Powell.

'One Nation' was, in effect, a continuation of the work of the Charters and represented the thoughts of progressive Conservatives now that they had become Members of Parliament. Critics described it as 'One Notion', that notion being Parliamentary self-advancement; but that was not justified. It was a clear indication to the old guard, which included Churchill, that the next Conservative Government would have to proceed on very different lines from its predecessors. One suspects that Churchill himself did not read it. When the Conservative Government of 1951 came to power he had reached the stage of not being able to recognise whom he had appointed as President of the Board of Trade and whom as Minister of Works. Although I know it will be regarded as blasphemy, I think he was, during that time, a very bad Prime Minister.

For those who wish to succeed in the House of Commons and are not content just to remain good constituency men on the back benches, it is essential to specialise. It is not wholly desirable to specialise in the subject on which they are employed outside the House of Commons, although it is sometimes important that they should make contributions on matters about which they have practical experience. This does tend to create the impression that they are hired representatives of a profession or trade. I personally seldom spoke on advertising or asked questions about it except on the occasion when monstrous attacks were made on advertising men during the passage of the Bill on commercial television. It was during the final debate on this subject that my former tutor, Patrick Gordon-Walker, distinguished himself by warning the House that as a result people would spend their time sitting at home twiddling their knobs. He was quite mystified at the hilarious reception this remark received. It is not surprising that he was not a great success as Minister of Education.

Another absurd occasion was the meeting at which those in favour of commercial television explained to the '1922 Committee' why it was desirable to establish it in order to break the monopoly of the B.B.C., and that it was essential to obtain the finance from a source other than increased licences and this could only be found in advertising. This was generally agreed. When it was all over one M.P. remarked, 'I'm in favour of it so long as we don't have any of these damned advertisements.' He never held office, although he strongly fancied himself as Secretary of State for War. Fortunately for the Army, who had already suffered under him as a brigadier, the leadership did not share his view.

Having just retired from the Territorial Army, I took up defence matters and in due course became Secretary of the Conservative Parliamentary Army Sub-Committee. I also became a member of the executive of the '1922 Committee' and subsequently its Secretary. The Parliamentary committee system operated by the political parties, as opposed to the official committees appointed by the House itself, changes in importance according to whether the Party is in power or in opposition. At all times the '1922 Committee' preserves its authority as the back-benchers committee. With the exception of the two secretaries, the officers are usually M.P.s who have no front-bench aspirations although this again depends on whether the Party is in power when their election takes place. The '1922 Committee' was formed in 1922 when the Party had been defeated. It is sometimes referred to in the Press as 'the all-powerful 1922 Committee' and on certain occasions its reactions can be of great importance. It is not a body which any Minister can take lightly. Even Churchill paid his respects to it.

In 1951 Labour went into the wilderness for thirteen years. In 1955 Churchill resigned and the heir-apparent, Anthony Eden, duly succeeded and had R. A. Butler at his right hand. The Eden story has been recorded at length elsewhere and it is not a very happy one. He was essentially the second-in-command who was not really fitted to command. When he was at Downing Street he could never forget that he was not still across the road at the Foreign Office. This was not well received by the diplomats and was not calculated to strengthen the position or the authority of the Foreign Secretary. He was essentially an old-Etonian type and he liked to have old-Etonian types around him. I was not such a person and I will not conceal the fact that I did not hold him in high regard.

Disaster came for Eden over Suez when he was exposed to violent attack in the House of Commons and in the Press against which he was not psychologically equipped to retaliate. He was immensely sensitive to criticism which is not a healthy thing for a Prime Minister or any Minister or for any Member of Parliament.

One of the advantages of having a constituency so near at hand was that I was able to play a full part in its affairs whilst the House was sitting. This is something which presents difficulties for those whose seats are far away from Westminster. In a marginal seat it is essential that the Member should not only be heard but should also be seen. An M.P. in the London area has the advantage of excellent press coverage in the London evening papers which are read by many of his constituents as they commute home. If he is sensible he will, from time to time, travel with them so that when they get home they can say casually in the pub, 'I had quite a chat with the Member on the train tonight.' It is also right that he should share with them the agonies of rush-hour travel on London Transport.

In Harrow East we improved our position steadily over the years, although I knew that it could never be regarded as a safe seat: a fact which was to escape the attention of my successor. I made a point of being in the constituency every week to hear the problems of my constituents. This procedure is generally called a surgery. I preferred to call it my consulting room as I have never cared for the sight of blood. I also made a regular report on Parliament which was regarded as a non-party occasion for the benefit of all members of the constituency. Few Socialists ever came but quite a number of Liberals did. I was also careful not to be seen to favour any particular element in the constituency and attended the Catholic church, the synogogue, the Methodist chapel and, of course, the Church of England on any occasion I was requested to do so.

My first public appearance after the General Election of 1950 was at the parish church in Stanmore, where, at that time, Attlee lived. He sat next to me. I confess that I did not pray for him. But then I doubt if he prayed for me. On the other hand I was sufficiently restrained not to pray for his defeat. I may add that I have never gone so far as to believe, as did one of my constituents, that God is on the side of the Conservatives. If you work it out that is no more ridiculous than believing that God is on either side in a war.

I was a great supporter of the British Legion and they always very kindly asked me to their annual dinner the Saturday before Remembrance Sunday. In view of what went on I always felt that this was tempting providence and that someone was almost bound to collapse on the march next day. It was always agreed that this was not an occasion for serious speaking and what was said was never reported. The Mayor of Harrow was a fellow guest one year and this fact had clearly not been conveyed to him. He took this moment to deliver a message to his fellow townsmen which somewhat astonished them. He ended by saying that he knew that I shared the pleasure of such occasions as it enabled us to come amongst 'our people'. This was too much and the speech of His Worship ended in a demonstration which was far from worshipful. Members of local authorities have a peculiar love of pomp which is quite unjustified by their circumstances.

In the course of attending to the needs of my constituents I became involved with one particular family whose record was quite remarkable. I will call them the X's. The husband had just come out of prison; his wife was being sued by the L.C.C. for selling papers illegally on Council property; the eldest daughter who was thirteen, was in the care of the local authority having been involved in a sexual affair with a man; the boy had been charged with committing homosexual offences. The final blow fell when they were charged with leaving their baby locked alone in an attic. It so happened that the charge by the L.C.C. was not properly founded and as a member of that august authority I endeavoured to persuade them to drop it. I failed, and so subsequently did they. I gained the eternal gratitude of the X's who plastered their house on the Council estate with blue posters. As it was well known that their house was frequented by people for distinctly blue purposes this terrified my agent and his agony was increased by the fact that Mr. X, who had by then become a bus conductor, spent the time announcing to his passengers that they must vote for Mr. Harvey, saying 'He's one of the family.' As the permissive society had not then come into being, this was not regarded as a good vote-catching exercise.

I recount these incidents in order to disprove the suggestion that the life of an M.P. is a dull one: mine certainly never was and whilst I was naturally concerned with influencing people I was also able to make many friends including, for better or for worse, the X's. That made life worth living.

During my years on the back benches I was never associated with any pressure groups, nor did I take any part in dissident activities. Those who become so involved sometimes do so for reasons of conscience. More often they are disgruntled because they have expected better of the leadership or they may seriously believe that they are on an ultimately winning ticket. Organisation men seldom behave like that and the Conservative organisation is basically establishment minded.

At one point I was involved in a clash with Barbara Castle, who was to prove one day to be the best man in the Wilson Government. On this occasion Mrs. Castle had delivered an attack on Sir Winston Churchill of whom she said, 'The Right Honourable gentleman was once regarded as a bulldog seated on the Union Jack: now he is nothing but a lap-dog sitting on the Stars and Stripes.' Speaking after her I observed that we all knew on which flag the Honourable Lady is sitting and 'she "is no dog" '. Mr. Ian

Mikardo, of all people, was quite upset. I did have the decency to offer her a drink in the smoking-room afterwards.

One of the most important tasks assigned to me was to serve on the Select Committee for the Reform of the Army and Air Force Acts. I had always thought that service conditions lagged seriously behind those of civilians which was no aid to recruitment and was, in any case, an unjustifiable state of affairs. Conservatives tended to believe that if men joined the services this was what they must expect. There is no need to argue about such stupidity. As a result of my views I often found myself in agreement with the Labour members of the Committee. Of these the most distinguished and well-informed was George Wigg. Both Churchill and Antony Head, the Secretary of State for War at that time, adopted a foolish attitude towards Wigg who was one of the few members of his party who really had the interests of the services at heart. They mocked at him for being an Education Corps colonel, whereas he had previously had a long career in the Tank Corps.

On one occasion it was reported to me by one of my spies at the War Office that the General in charge of the military team, which gave evidence before us, had declared that I was a secret Communist. This was due to the fact that I had insisted that young men on National Service should not be permitted to sign up on a regular basis without the permission of their parents. I knew that they were liable to recruitment whilst under the influence of either drink or the sergeant-major or both. In defence of the General concerned I must state that the evidence given by him and his staff was extremely comprehensive and efficient. It was amusing, when we came to reform the Air Force Act, to note the difference. I sometimes thought I knew more about the Air Force than they did. This is no doubt the sort of inter-service prejudice which I have always deplored. I did in fact get into trouble with the Navy when I asked at Question Time when the Navy Act was to be reformed in order to bring that reactionary service into line. The ex-sailors in the House, who had as much sense of humour as they had intelligence, were furious. That was a Select Committee on which I was not asked to serve. It was not surprising that the *Scharnhorst* and *Gneisenau* got through.

When Suez came there were a number of resignations by Conservative Ministers and I was sent for by Anthony Eden, largely I think on the advice of Edward Heath who was then Deputy Chief

Whip. He told me that he would like me to go as Parliamentary Secretary at the Ministry of Supply. I felt it my duty to point out to him that I was on record as having said that the Ministry of Supply ought to be wound up. He seemed unperturbed by the revelation and observed that I would in any case be useful speaking in the country. This seemed to me to be a *non sequitur*. Nevertheless I accepted.

I always felt much the same about Suez as I did about Munich. Whilst I did not regard it as a commendable decision I thought that in the circumstances it was the only possible one. Those circumstances emanated from our withdrawing troops from the Suez Canal and were explained at the meeting of the Conservative Parliamentary Defence Committee, at which I put up the maps. Having made that mistake it was up to us to demand that Nasser withdraw within twenty-four hours 'or else'. This was not done primarily because there was no 'or else'. We had also to consider the implications of the Russian contribution to the Aswan Dam which we had foolishly left open for them to make. Consequently the matter dithered on until the Labour Opposition, which under Gaitskell had originally supported the Government, had seen the advantages of changing ground and the disadvantages of staying put.

The lessons of Suez are clear. One is the danger of making false appreciations and the other is the damage done as a result of having no clear objective. Both are disastrous to the effective conduct of foreign policy. The false appreciation of 1956 was based on the assumption that the withdrawal of troops from the Canal would be compensated for by the British presence in Cyprus and that in any case Eygpt would honour her obligations under the renewed Canal agreement. Both these conclusions were contested by the Conservative 'Suez Group' in the House of Commons who were proved right. The conception of a military presence is a dangerous one if it is inadequate for the task. It can lead to escalation and to withdrawal with the resulting loss of face. To lose face in the Middle and Far East is an unpardonable indiscretion.

It was never clear whether the objective of the British Government was to restore the *status quo*, to force Nasser to make a new agreement which was acceptable to the *amour propre* of the Egyptian people, or to overthrow him. The outcome of the operation was the virtual destruction of what remained of British prestige in the Middle East. Anglo-American relations were seriously damaged. Soviet influence in the area increased and the Egyptians were encouraged to believe in a military prowess which they did not possess and which took the Six Days War to remove.

The deplorable display of internecine warfare which took place in the House of Commons destroyed Anthony Eden and emphasised the desirability of establishing a bi-partisan foreign policy. The failure to do this is one of the weaknesses of any democracy, especially in view of the fact that in contending with the Communists they are confronted by a régime which tolerates no such internal arguments. To achieve this demands concessions on both sides and the acceptance of a general consensus. This was not present at Suez. It has not been achieved since owing to conflicting ideologies, divided objectives, and differing methods. All these affect in varying proportions Britain's dealings with other countries, her role in the world, her associations with the Commonwealth, the organisation of her defence forces and the conduct of overseas information, which is the polite word for propaganda.

Whilst all this was drawing to its close I was at the Ministry of Supply. My period there was neither long nor distinguished but it was very pleasant and gave me an undisturbed tenure on the Front Bench which was to be denied me in the days ahead. Maudling was the Minister and he was essentially calm and unruffled : not that he had much cause to be otherwise. He too was to experience a change of affairs in the future but it did not affect him, at least not outwardly. He, like myself, believed that the Ministry should be absorbed into the other service Ministries. It had been created as part of the wartime machinery when it had a very considerable part to play. But, after all, the war had been over ten years although there had always been the threat of another one if the Russians proved difficult over Germany. To have two Ministers who believed that they ought to be abolished must have been discouraging for the civil servants in the Ministry, but they all behaved impeccably which was a lesson to me.

At the end of 1956 it was clear that Eden could no longer go on. He was a sick man, both physically and mentally, and he retired to the Bahamas to recuperate : not exactly the place for a commanding general in battle. The question of a successor then arose. When Baldwin, Chamberlain and Churchill had gone the situation had been different. The decision rested with the Cabinet : no one would have considered consulting the junior Ministers, let alone the 'all-powerful 1922 Committee'. Had this all occurred a year before it seems probable that Butler would have got the job. During Suez Butler had behaved in a somewhat odd way. In the House he said nothing to indicate that he did not support Anthony Eden. Outside it, and in the presence of the Press, he gave a very different impression. He had become 'Mr. Facing Both Ways' and for those who believed in him and were grateful for the contribution he had made to the thinking of the Party this was sad. It was not unreasonable that he should have been personally irritated by the antics of Suez. As far as one can make out he was not in the inner circle, which consisted of Eden, Macmillan, Lloyd and Head. It was interesting that the Socialists never made much of the fact that Macmillan had been involved in this way after he became Prime Minister, but then all the Cabinet had been involved officially.

Butler also damaged himself by his aloofness. He seldom came into the smoking-room and hardly ever spoke to his junior colleagues. When the leadership question was on the horizon he suddenly appeared, but it was then looked on as a joke. I had been astonished some while before when I was dining alone in the Carlton Club waiting for my first daughter to be born when he came and joined me. He talked at great length and was very amusing and extremely indiscreet. It made my evening.

On one occasion when Aubrey Jones was answering questions in the House with some difficulty, Butler suddenly got up and marched out muttering loudly that he could not stand any more of it. But this was after the leadership struggle was over and he was not to know that it was not the last such struggle in which he was to be involved. He always seemed strangely unappreciative of his original team who had all 'arrived', and people noticed this.

When the Conservative hierarchy decided on Macmillan it must have been a sad blow for Butler. Macmillan had never been as close to the leadership as he had. At the same time many of the things that Macmillan had said and written before the war were as progressive as the ideas which Butler incorporated in the Charters. Macmillan was very much a dark horse. Despite my high regard for Butler I was nevertheless satisfied that Macmillan was the right man for the post of Prime Minister in what was for the Conservatives a crisis.

Whereas Anthony Eden was essentially a diplomat first and a politician second, Macmillan was equally a politician and a diplomat. He understood people and he cared about them. He knew that politicians who pretended to be ordinary were not respected by the electorate. But he also knew that the electorate distrusted ostentatiously clever people. *The Middle Way*, the title of his prewar book which many people have never read, was a truly representative title for him. He was never afraid of change and he welcomed experiment. He was acceptable to all sections of the Party, although when he became Prime Minister many people outside politics scarcely knew him. He loved panache and he knew that the British people loved it too, even if they did not know the meaning of the word. In some senses he was an enigma and that made him all the more interesting. He was never dull and he was not only a good talker but also a good listener. Above all he understood the make-up of the Conservative Party and although he was highly intelligent treated stupid people kindly, and there were plenty about in the political field.

It was for these reasons that I believed he was the right choice for Prime Minister and not merely because of the early days when he had supported me at the Oxford Union, or because he had come especially to speak for me at Harrow East. On that occasion he greatly alarmed my agent at the end of his speech by saying that he hoped that everyone present would vote for me. As the General Election had not yet been announced this meant that according to electoral law we had started our campaign and all expenses thereafter had to be declared. Eden went to the country a week later so we were saved having to fight the election on a shoe-string.

Macmillan sent me to the Foreign Office as Joint Parliamentary Under-Secretary under Selwyn Lloyd. I had the particular duty of supervising Information Services. In this I had to liaise closely with Charles Hill, who had become Chancellor of the Duchy of Lancaster and was in charge of all government information. He had asked me before he took over his duties to let him have my views on the function he had been requested to undertake. I gave him a short paper based on my commercial experience as the head of public relations of W. S. Crawford Ltd., from which I had had to resign when I went to the Ministry of Supply.

I made the point that he must insist on being a member of the

Cabinet. I knew, from having dealt with the tycoons of industry, that they are only likely to call on those who deal with public relations problems when they think they need them, and this is invariably too late. In a sense this was exactly what happened in January 1957 when Suez was over and the damage had been done. Charles Hill was expected to pick up the bits and to restore the health of the Government, a role for which the famous radio doctor was adjudged to be well equipped. That done it was more than probable that he would have been relegated to limbo until another crisis arose were he not in a position of authority as one of the policy-makers.

I pointed out in my note that he must be given full authority to co-ordinate all Information Services, both at home and overseas, and if necessary control them and use his veto. If he had to deal with senior Ministers it was essential that he should be one himself. I had little doubt that this proposal would be commended by him; fortunately it was also approved by Harold Macmillan.

The appointment of Charles Hill to this position with these powers was not well received by the Press. They thought he would erect a barrier between themselves and other Ministers and that information would be subject to continuous censorship which would interfere with their work. This never happened. In fact under his guidance and that of his assistant, Harold Evans, information flowed more freely than it had done before. The other Ministries did not welcome his appointment because they thought that it could mean interference from outside. This seldom occurred, although the Navy was once prevented by him from circulating a film to the fleet which demonstrated indubitably that Suez was not a failure because of the action of the services but because of the ineptitude of the politicians. This was largely true, but was not exactly what was required in restoring the confidence of the nation in its leaders. The Sea Lords were most indignant at this decision and appealed to Macmillan, who, not surprisingly, upheld it.

Information was not highly regarded at the Foreign Office at that time. Many of the information officers were not permanent members of the service and it was thought to be a handicap to one's diplomatic career to be assigned to an information post. My first act was to ask for the appointment of a new Assistant Under-Secretary to be in charge of information as the existing incumbent was wearied by his experience of Suez and his heart was not in his work. I did not blame him and I was not surprised that my request was readily granted. I was fortunate to have Ralph Murray as his successor, a man who understood the subject perfectly and who had experience at the B.B.C. where he is now a Governor since retiring as our Ambassador in Greece.

Anthony Eden, upset by the broadcasts by the B.B.C. during the Suez crisis, had insisted that a Foreign Office official should be stationed at Broadcasting House to vet overseas news. This was understandably greatly resented by Sir Ian Jacob, the Chairman, and his staff. The unfortunate individual had a miserable time and was practically spat at in the corridors. It was an arrangement of which I totally disapproved and with Selwyn Lloyd's approval I had him removed. But it took us a long time to restore good relations with the B.B.C. and it was largely due to Ralph Murray that this was done as quickly as it was.

Although I had never had any diplomatic experience, and few junior Ministers who go to the Foreign Office ever have, I did not find it all that difficult to understand the nature of the requirements of the Information Services. My training as an advertising man had taught me the basic factors in dealing with people and I always had in mind the saying of an old colleague, 'Bingy' Saxon-Mills: 'Never state without communicating.'

Information in its political context involves all the forms of communication. Publicity, public relations, campaign promotion, and the mounting of exhibitions all come under this umbrella title. So does the dissemination of news; so too does propaganda.

An American writer has said that 'propaganda' is a good word gone wrong. In British eyes it went particularly wrong under the control of Dr. Goebbels. Yet nothing the Nazi cripple did equalled in scope, technique, or in its total disregard for morality and truth, the subsequent operations of international Communism as directed by the Soviet Union. Furthermore, the activities of Goebbels in the international sphere were singularly unsuccessful taken by themselves. They prevailed only under conditions where the full force of a police state was present or where they were sustained in the background by the armed power of the Nazi Third Reich.

The same is by no means true of Communist propaganda. Its influence in the world has grown steadily since 1945. Unlike the Nazi effusion it is not regarded as the product of a megalomaniac. On occasions it has been sustained, albeit unintentionally, by the conduct of politicians, Press and leaders of public opinion in the very countries which it seeks to destroy. Even more ironical is the fact that it is the so-called intellectuals who have, by their opposition to any form of effective retaliation, performed this service.

The primary task of information is to present policy, or a particular aspect of policy, in such a way as to command the maximum support both at home and abroad. Its second task is to refute, directly or by inference, by overt means or secrecy, the opposition case. In carrying out these tasks every appropriate instrument of communication must be used within the resources available. Finally there must be a correct assessment of the psychological make-up of those to whom the approach is made. The greatest single cause of failure of information in any sphere is the use of the wrong approach : in fact statement without communication.

Information is therefore an instrument of policy. It is not a substitute for it, nor can it function effectively when there is no clearly defined policy line. Therefore it is of great importance that the advisers on information, who are responsible for the presentation of policy, should be kept fully in the picture. It was on this conclusion that I had based my advice to Charles Hill. The task of projection, the preparing of the ground before the announcement of a policy decision, is in many ways more important than the measures taken afterwards to ensure its general acceptance and to off-set critical analysis.

It was with these thoughts in mind that I approached my task. For a professional publicity man they were not particularly original thoughts, but I found a peculiar reluctance to having them accepted in practice at the highest level. One distinguished Foreign Office official, a Wykehamist, once told me that he did not believe in information. He was essentially a secret diplomatist who would have got on well with Metternich. I must admit, nevertheless, that I was in agreement with him when it came to the business of 'summitry' which achieved little and played into the hands of the Communists, who were far better at that sort of theatrical gimmick.

It was this particular diplomat, for whom I had in every other respect a great regard, who rang me up when I was in the bath and brought me dripping to the telephone to tell me that the Japanese Foreign Secretary whom I was preparing to escort to the theatre had just been insulted on television by some person called Day. When I asked him what he suggested I should do about it he said he thought it would be helpful if I were to ring up the editor of *The Times* and ask him not to refer to the matter in his columns. I could hardly believe my ears. Apart from the fact that it was unlikely that the editor would have heard about the incident and the paper had already gone to bed, this was exactly the sort of conduct that the Press had anticipated when the Charles Hill team had gone into action. Had I been so insane as to comply with this request it would most certainly have insured that the story would have been prominently featured. I remarked that this was the sort of information in which I did not believe. He took it very well. He subsequently became a most successful Ambassador to Portugal where no doubt he found an ally in Dr. Salazar.

The occasion of the visit of the Japanese Foreign Secretary displayed an interesting side of the Foreign Office mentality to me. When I was instructed to undertake this particular mission I discovered that we could not go to Covent Garden, a popular venue for such occasions, as the Chinese Ballet were performing there. The next alternative, Sadlers Wells, was closed. It was not thought suitable to go to a straight play as it might not be fully understood and, having seen some of them, I agreed. So I suggested that it might be an exciting innovation to go to see the dogs at the White City. This was received with horror and I was politely informed that this would be regarded by the Japanese as an insult to their cultural integrity. So we had to settle for *Hamlet* at the Old Vic, which did not please me as I had had enough of the Prince of Denmark, having seen him at his best with Gielgud and at his worst with Glenville. The Japanese were polite but unenthusiastic and I managed to stay awake until the bitter end. John Neville was neither brilliant like Gielgud nor funny like Glenville. Afterwards we went on to the Savoy where the floor show was decidedly 'blue' and quite shocked my P.A. who was a very respectable young man from Wimbledon. The Japanese loved every minute of it and insisted on staying until the end which was at two o'clock in the morning. I am sure they would have enjoyed the dogs, and the Foreign Office officials would have got to bed by midnight. Although not a word was said about the person called Day it was not, I think, without significance that the Japanese Ambassador who must have condoned the interview, was recalled shortly afterwards.

The Foreign Service has been subjected to many attacks by politicians and the Press, so I feel that I should place on record that I believe we have the finest diplomatic service in the world, and its achievements far outweigh the mistakes which have been made from time to time. In the short period I was there I formed the highest opinion of the intelligence and integrity of the officials at all levels and of their dedication to their work – even those who did not believe in information.

It is extremely dubious whether it is wise to appoint non-members of the Foreign and Colonial Service to high ambassadorial positions. Admittedly where these appointments have been made they have been successful, such as Halifax and Harlech in Washington, Soames in Paris and Hoare in Madrid. But now that the service is contracting this is not encouraging for the middle grades who see their chances of promotion threatened. Neither is it likely to improve the possibilities of recruiting young and able men for the service. This is hardly calculated to strengthen the authority of Britain's voice in the world or to improve Commonwealth relations.

At just about the time that I arrived at my desk the *Daily Mirror* published a booklet entitled 'Britain's Voice Abroad' which was intended as an attack on our Information Services. It was extremely well written and I asked the author, Michael King, who was a political correspondent and also the son of Cecil Harmsworth King, to come to see me. I congratulated him on his work which I said would be of great assistance to me. As a result of this exchange I was invited to lunch with the great man himself. It was a very hot day and we lunched under a glass roof in the old *Daily Mirror* building. There were only the three of us. It was rather like being summoned by God or at any rate a rehearsal for that occasion if it ever occurs. I was told afterwards that I had not made a great impression : and in that I was in good company. On the other hand he impressed me greatly. I endeavoured, despite this setback, to continue with my work.

One of the most important tasks of the Under-Secretary's office was to prepare the answers to Parliamentary Questions. In many respects the Parliamentary Question is one of the most effective instruments for defending the private citizen's own interests. It is possible, by using them correctly, to penetrate the defences of the most obdurate Ministry and to bring to light cases of injustice and incompetence. Therefore it is unfortunate that certain M.P.s treat it as a useful way of getting personal publicity by asking what are sometimes totally irrelevant questions. A great deal of time is also wasted by inane and lengthy supplementary questions which prevent more important matters being raised on the floor of the House. The public should take note of these offenders in the light of the great expense involved in answering questions, not to mention Ministers' time and that of their Ministries.

Questions to the Foreign Secretary are particularly difficult, as I had good reason to learn, because they often touch on areas which are diplomatically sensitive and are also on the borders of security. An unguarded reply to a carefully aimed supplementary by the opposition may lead to an international reaction and to calls from angry Ambassadors. There was the notable occasion when the Minister of State at the Colonial Office was asked when he expected Cyprus to be granted her sovereignty. To this he sharply replied 'Never'. He was soon to be kicked upstairs.

Selwyn Lloyd did not really care for Parliamentary Questions. He was not in fact at his best in the House of Commons. It was unfortunate for him that he was confronted by Aneurin Bevan, who was a master of political debate and of the rapier thrust. He could also be extremely amusing. He once nearly got me into grave trouble when I was sitting next to Selwyn Lloyd and he made his famous remark: 'Why attack the monkey when the organ-grinder's here?' It was all I could do not to burst out laughing. In the House of Commons it is useful to have a sense of humour but there are occasions when it can be dangerous.

Selwyn Lloyd was nevertheless an able Foreign Secretary. He was not afraid of any attack that was made upon him and there were many after Suez. He did not bear malice but he had a good memory. Gladwyn Jebb was said to have called him a 'bell-hop' when Eden was Prime Minister. Jebb did not become the head of the Foreign Service but had to content himself with a Liberal peerage. When I appointed a new P.A. to succeed the young gentleman from Wimbledon I told him that when he was dealing with the Foreign Secretary he should never pretend to know something he did not, and that he should never be frightened of the somewhat austere countenance which I have often thought slightly resembles Oliver Cromwell's. My P.A. carried my second piece of advice to extreme by laughing when Selwyn had suggested a somewhat absurd answer to a Parliamentary question. Selwyn was not amused and the senior

Foreign Office officlials who were present pretended to be shocked, although they must have sympathised with the reaction. I was delighted. I detest 'yes-men'. I have little doubt that my P.A. will one day become a top Ambassador.

When I went to the Foreign Office Selwyn was not popular with the diplomats as a result of Suez about which few of them had been consulted. They knew that I was a Selwyn Lloyd man and they were careful not to show this when I was around. In any case they had been correctly taught to be careful of all politicians.

There were two Ministers of State at the Foreign Office, Alan Noble and David Ormsby-Gore, who was later to become Lord Harlech. My counterpart in the House of Lords was Lord Gosford, a charming but bewildered peer who had originally been drafted as Lord Salisbury's assistant, but the noble Lord had had one of his resigning fits and Gosford was left to carry the can. It was unkindly said by the Foreign Office juniors that Selwyn had forgotten Gosford. This got me into trouble one evening when I went to a Foreign Office reception, at which the Foreign Secretary was receiving, and I introduced him to Gosford who was with me. This was another of the occasions when Selwyn was not amused. He was not amused either when he was writing a speech at three o'clock in the morning and I fell asleep on the sofa and snored. David Ormsby-Gore had to kick my ankle to wake me up. Still, it was something to be kicked by a future Ambassador to the United States.

In my capacity as Under-Secretary I was Chairman of the Committee concerned with the British Pavilion at the Brussels Exhibition of 1958. At my first meeting with the Committee some young man from an advertising agency of which I had never heard gave me a lecture on the importance of advertising. I never saw him again, which was odd. Our official representative was Sir John Balfour, a distinguished ex-Ambassador who was a highly entertaining person and quite the best man for the job. Our pavilion was outstandingly good and the entrance was so impressive that people took off their hats when they entered, as if they were going into church. One day while it was under construction 'Jock' Balfour came to me in a great state of agitation : the Fishmongers Company who owned the Annigoni portrait of the Queen which we wanted to hang in the main hall had refused to let it go out of the country. I called for alternative suggestions and was amazed when the

Foreign Office suggested that, as a member of Christ Church, I might persuade them to let us have the portrait of Henry VIII which is in the hall at Oxford. I pointed out, as a humble non-diplomat, that this might not be well received by the Catholics in Belgium. They admitted that I had a point, so we eventually decided to have a reproduction of the Annigoni. Sir John Balfour complained that he did not think that the *cognoscenti* would approve, but I assured him that these would be few in number. After enduring two months of the exhibition he agreed with me.

I was unfortunately prevented from attending the opening of the exhibition by catching chicken-pox from my children which turned into double pneumonia and nearly killed me.

One of the most arduous and thankless, not to mention dangerous, tasks in the Information side of the Foreign Office is that of the Foreign Office spokesman. He gets credit for little that goes right and blame for everything that goes wrong, from both inside and outside. I was fortunate in having a dedicated man in charge of it called Peter Hope who I am glad to say has since become an Ambassador. It was his duty to meet the Press at regular intervals during the day and also to deal with the non-believers in information in the office. He handled all of them with great skill. It was over one of his statements that I had my only occasion to doubt the wisdom of Harold Macmillan. The Prime Minister was asked about some Foreign Office statement and was unable to give the answer as he had not read it, which was not unreasonable. He thereupon issued an order that the Foreign Office spokesman should never issue statements without the authority of the Foreign Secretary or, in his absence, No. 10. This was an absurd request and implied that the department in general, and I in particular, could not be trusted. I went so far as to demand the cancellation of this order and I got my way.

Another little fracas occurred with my friend and colleague at the Treasury, the redoubtable Enoch Powell. One morning Ralph Murray, who was the epitome of composure, arrived at my office in the nearest to a state of alarm that I had ever seen and showed me a questionnaire from Enoch demanding details of Foreign Office expenditure on information. The nature of some of this was what is called 'black' and would not be allowed outside the Foreign Office. I took the questionnaire, drew my pen through every page and wrote: 'Mind your own business. Love Ian'. I then went to

Selwyn to warn him to expect a call from the Chancellor, Peter Thorneycroft, which duly came through. It was my contention, and Selwyn supported me in it, that once a financial allocation had been made by the Treasury and approved by the Cabinet the way the money was then spent was a matter for the department concerned. It was over this kind of issue that Thorneycroft, Nigel Birch and Powell subsequently resigned but I make no claim to having precipitated the matter.

I went on three tours of inspection of our Information Services overseas during my term of office. The first was to Germany in January of 1958, which was very cold. It was only a few weeks before the Munich air disaster. I went to Bonn and looked across the river to Bad Godesberg with all its memories of that other Munich. I also went to Berlin and was astonished at the difference between the gaiety of West Berlin and the drabness of East Berlin: there was no wall then. Subsequently I remarked on this in a conversation with the Polish Ambassador in London. He made the rather strange observation that the Russians had to allow this otherwise it would cause discontent in Eastern Germany. This appeared to me to be openly admitting the differences in the conditions prevailing in the much vaunted D.D.R. and those in the imperialist-capitalist Federal Republic. He was not prepared to comment further when pressed and I did not blame him as the room was no doubt bugged.

My second trip was to the U.S.A. where our relations after Suez were still not good. Senator Cabot Lodge, whom I have loathed since, had turned his back on Piers Dixon at the United Nations. Fortunately I did not have to meet him. The United States at that time were still under the impression that they were ordained by God to save the world from Communism. There is now some evidence to the contrary. At that time they were not in the midst of their racial troubles. I have always found it difficult to understand that a nation who had declared all men equal was able to pursue such an attitude towards coloured citizens. I am sure God did not ordain that. There is now even more evidence to the contrary. In the field of foreign policy the American administration has always suffered from having one political voice and one commercial voice and from having Ministers who have both. The result is confusion worse confounded. Nevertheless, despite any impression to the contrary, I remain unquestionably pro-American.

In New York I found the redoubtable Bill Ormerod, who was a highly respected and popular personality. The walls of his office were covered with the photographs of his distinguished friends. His contacts were universal. With him I attended one of the most enjoyable evenings of my life when Rogers and Hammerstein performed a selection of their works and Mary Martin sang. I also found myself the unexpected guest of the Harvard Delphic Club dinner. I was made an honorary member of the Club when I went to the Harvard Tercentenary Celebrations before the war. I made a speech and was mistaken for Selwyn Lloyd, so it was altogether a hilarious occasion.

I found San Francisco one of the most attractive cities I have ever visited and Los Angeles the most vulgar. In San Francisco I created a stir by making a speech in which I said that if America's policy towards China was more realistic their harbour would be less empty. Immediately telegrams arrived from the Foreign Office demanding to know exactly what I had said and why. I thought for a moment that I would be recalled, but that would have drawn even more attention to the incident. The people in San Francisco obviously agreed with me, but in Washington they were less enthusiastic.

The Foreign Office was always worried about my speeches, when I was allowed to make them, ever since the day I arrived at a luncheon and was handed a paper with my speech already written. I threw it in the wastepaper-basket, saying that I wrote my own speeches and would ask for assistance when I needed it. On one occasion they were most perturbed when I was about to open a conference at Wilton Park attended by a number of German ex-generals. Wilton Park was an establishment which was designed to teach the Germans how to become democrats. How far it succeeded time alone will show. During the war it had been a Divisional Headquarters and was very much in the potential invasion area. I had remarked on this to the Foreign Office and indicated that I would remind the generals. They were particularly alarmed because the German Ambassador was to be present. I persevered and when welcoming our ex-opponents said that the last time I had been there I had been waiting for them but they had not turned up. Now it was a pleasure to see them. They all laughed heartily, including the Ambassador, and the Foreign Office officials breathed again.

Sir Harold Caccia was our Ambassador in Washington. He was extremely athletic and made me play tennis throughout one hot afternoon. I had not played for years and when his staff had retired to dress for dinner he insisted on a last single. Fortunately I was extremely fit, which no doubt astonished him in a politician. I don't think many of my colleagues, with the notable exception of Ernest Marples, would have survived. I found Caccia immensely well informed and very well disposed to help over our information work which he subsequently did. I even persuaded him that it would be a good thing if Ormerod were to have a knighthood, although he was not a permanent official. The Foreign Office rather gibbed at this and suggested that it would be best to wait until he retired. I told them that the Americans preferred active knights to decayed ones and they gave way. In those days it was not normal to give M.B.E.s to people like the Beatles or accolades to the princes of sport, so my suggestion was considered a trifle bizarre.

My third tour was of Spain, Italy, Jugoslavia and Austria. In Rome I had an amusing interchange in the American Information centre which was a very grand place compared with our own British Council offices, although it was practically empty and ours was jam-packed. The American conception that you can buy anything with money dies hard. I asked a young man why he was in the service and he replied that he had been in business where he had failed miserably, then he had tried law where he had done the same, and then he had had a nervous breakdown and so here he was. His superiors were not at all pleased and hurried me away.

On our way from Rome to Belgrade we landed in a field behind Dubrovnik and were greeted by a number of cows, and then, narrowly missing the mountains behind, we swept into a terrifying thunderstorm and were nearly struck by lightning in what was a very old and draughty Dakota of the Jugoslav airlines. In Austria I found Noel-Baker, known to Selwyn Lloyd as 'the wet lettuce', on his way to a conference. I thought that as he was an ex-Cabinet Minister I had better be polite and I escorted him to the station where we put him on the wrong train. This was only discovered just in time. I am sure he thought I had done it intentionally and, had I thought of it, I have no doubt that I would have done.

I paid one other visit abroad which was only partly a Foreign Office duty. This was to Ghana. There I met Nkrumah, whom I found fascinating. He had not at that moment committed some of his more gross offences or at least he had not been found out. At the dinner to celebrate the occasion I sat at his right hand whilst the French representative, who was black, sat on his left. As the Frenchman could not speak English and Nkrumah could not speak French he devoted all his attention to me and we laughed a great deal. It was most stimulating. My officials were greatly impressed. A few years later I should no doubt have been labelled as pro-Fascist.

Geoffrey Byng, whom I had known in the House of Commons as Labour M.P. for Hornchurch, was the Attorney-General at the time. I spent a morning alone with him when we went to see the new harbour at Tema and drank neat whisky on the way. This alarmed my officials, who thought that it was dangerous for me to be alone with him and wanted to come with us. But I gave them the morning off.

I had an exhausting lunch with the Botsios. I had remarked to Botsio, one of Nkrumah's chief Ministers, that I found the food in the sumptuous Ambassador Hotel rather like that of the Grand Hotel at Eastbourne which had disappointed me. Mrs. Botsio thereupon gave me a typical Ghanaian lunch. The little rock crabs were delicious but the main course looked rather like engine oil with lumps of putty in it. Good manners demanded that I finished my immense helping and when I was not looking another equally large one was piled on my plate. At the end I demanded to be allowed to sleep it off in my hotel only to be reminded that I was due to make a broadcast in half an hour. I have no notion of what I said, but as there were no Foreign Office telegrams it must have been innocuous. I must, for once, have read my official brief.

Despite all these antics the Foreign Office treated me with great kindness and tolerance and I shall always be grateful to them for that. They were highly qualified people and must have found it difficult to deal with so unskilled a person. They were somewhat disturbed when I accepted a lunch with Malik, the Soviet Ambassador, all on my own. I found him most agreeable. When I arrived we had drinks and I took vodka. Having seen this drunk in all the best films about Russia, I dashed mine down in a single gulp whilst he proceeded to sip his as if it were sherry. I was not allowed to go to the Hungarian National Day celebrations at their Embassy by myself. As we were upset by their treatment of the Hungarian rising I was told that I must merely go in, shake hands, take one drink, eat nothing and leave at once. I found this a highly ridiculous way of going on and said so. But I did as I was told despite the caviar, and came away feeling a complete idiot. My escort was greatly relieved. He too has since become a top Ambassador.

My associations with Charles Hill were always entertaining. The Foreign Office regarded his activities with the greatest suspicion and were quite relieved that I was at hand to talk to him. We had a regular meeting every week which was attended by the P.R.O.s, or information officers as they were called, from all the Ministries. With a few exceptions they were not an inspiring lot. Very few of them appeared to have access to their Ministers and, if they had, I doubt if they contributed much to the discussion. They certainly contributed little to ours. When I left the Foreign Office I was in the process of trying to get a closer relationship established between the P.R.O.s in the Civil Service and those in commercial practice. It is something our new 'quiet revolutionaries' should consider.

I was also a member of the Conservative Liaison Committee which met once a week in Charles Hill's room and which considered publicity activities between the Government and the Party. Quintin Hogg was in the chair. The competition for leading the discussion between him and Charles Hill provided me with much material for stirring up the proceedings. Quintin had been opposed to the establishment of the I.T.A., so when the anniversary of its birth came round I suggested that we should issue a party leaflet outlining its achievement and underlining the fact that, but for us, it would not have come into being. I knew that Charles Hill would support this and that Quintin would oppose it. The leaflet was never published. It was all good clean fun.

Although Selwyn Lloyd had a rough time in the House of Commons, he was greeted with applause every time he spoke at the Party Conference. Apart from the fact that he spoke well, I think they felt they ought to repay him for all he went through in the interests of the cause. I had always taken an active part at Party Conferences both as a prospective candidate and as a Member of Parliament and I knew the ropes. It became my duty to accompany him on these occasions and I went both to Brighton in 1957 and Blackpool in 1958.

It was on the latter occasion that I was involved, as most people were in their time, in an argument with Randolph Churchill, whose main handicap was his name. He once fought a seat against Malcolm Macdonald and is reported to have said that no one would ever have heard of him if he had not been called Macdonald. Randolph had so much intelligence that I doubt whether this anecdote is true; he may, of course, have said it against himself, but this I very much doubt.

At Blackpool Selwyn had just put the finishing touches to his speech for the next morning and while we were having dinner in the conference hotel Randolph appeared from the bar and demanded to have a preview of the speech. As he was then writing for the *Evening Standard* which did not come out until after the speech there was no harm in his seeing it. In any case it contained no world-shattering pronouncements. Randolph accompanied us back to Selwyn's suite and perching himself with some difficulty on a pouffe he proceeded to read the speech, uttering bombastic expressions throughout. Finally he rose and thundered: 'Selwyn, no wonder you are such a flop when you allow these Foreign Office idiots to write your speeches. You should sack the lot.' The only Foreign Office idiot who had had any say at all in the document was myself, as it was strictly against the rules for any government official to have anything to do with party affairs. I pointed this out to Randolph, who pretended not to know who I was and abused me roundly. So I took him away and gave him a double brandy in the bar, which deterred him from molesting Selwyn further. The speech was a triumph and was accorded a five-minute ovation which annoyed Duncan Sandys who had just spoken and had only been given a polite round of applause. I felt that we had got our own back on the Churchillians.

By this time the 'Class of 1950' was emerging in positions of authority on the front bench. The most successful were Iain Macleod, Reginald Maudling, and Edward Heath. At that stage I would have ranked them in that order if it had been a question of nominating a future leader of the party. But history makes men and men make history. Few, if any, would have predicted in 1945 that Harold Macmillan would be the leader eleven years later, and fewer still that Alec Douglas-Home would succeed him.

Iain Macleod was at school with me at Fettes. He was a strange mixture of the romantic Highlander and the down-to-earth Scot. He was a man of penetrating intelligence. He was both ruthless and ambitious and he never made the mistake of wanting to be loved. As a speaker he had the ability both to stir the emotions and to appeal to the intellect. In the House of Commons he could be both cruel and amusing and he had the skill of instant repartee. Lord Salisbury, who had many of the qualities of the Cecils, did him irreparable damage when he described him as 'too clever by half'. I myself told him, when we were returning together from a political reception, that we both suffered from the same disease. This perturbed him and he asked me what I meant. I replied that neither of us suffered fools gladly and that the day might come when we would need their support and we should not get it. I was to be proved right.

Apart from that Iain Macleod made few mistakes, although it can be argued that it was an error of judgement to undertake the leadership of the House of Commons and the Chairmanship of the Party at the same time, but that was not entirely his decision. He was a man of courage both physically and mentally. His policy towards Africa at the Colonial Office undoubtedly destroyed his chances of the leadership: it alarmed too many members of the Party because it was in advance of its time. But he was not afraid to pursue it because he thought it was right although he knew it would do him no good. That made him a statesman and not just a top politician.

When the contest for the leadership arose he would not allow his name to go forward. He was too good a bridge-player to believe that it was a game he could still win. Had the battle between Heath and Maudling ended in a draw he might have been called upon, but that was not to happen. The television medium did not suit him, partly because his physical handicap tended to make him look sinister and partly because he was sometimes too rough with his opponents. Like Churchill he would have been a good war leader. He was to the end a great Conservative in the modern idiom. His premature death, which was largely caused by caring more about his work than himself, was a serious blow to the Party and to the Government which never needed his talents so much, as time will undoubtedly show.

Reginald Maudling has been described as lazy and lumbering and he has done little to dispel this accusation. In fact he has sometimes given the impression that it rather appeals to him. It makes him different; it also implies that he is steady and reliable. That is

D

certainly true. There is in fact something of the Baldwinesque about him. He is, moreover, both intelligent and liberal-minded. Had the leadership contest come at a time when the Party was in power he could well have been the victor: some people believe that if he had given more encouragement to his supporters to go out and fight for him he could have beaten Heath. But his general lack of exertion gave the impression that he would be less fitted to lead them back out of the wilderness. Unlike Heath and Macleod he was never a success at Party Conferences because he never roused them, which was largely due to the fact that he never roused himself. His were the tactics of 'softly, softly catchee monkey': unfortunately the tactics were too soft and the monkey went up another tree.

I first met Edward Heath at Oxford in the Union and, apart from our differences of opinion over Munich, we agreed on the future path the Conservative Party ought to follow, and I have never since differed from him. Had I been an M.P. at the time I would have voted for him as leader. After Oxford we met briefly during the war and then afterwards we saw a good deal of each other when we were in search of a seat. In fact we were both on the short list for Bexley, but I got Harrow East before they made their choice.

I know of no one who worked harder for the Party in those days and later when he was in the House. I suspect that three weekends out of four he had speaking engagements. Occasionally on a Sunday evening he would come and play the piano with my wife who once had aspirations to sing in opera and had studied at the Royal College of Music.

As Chief Whip he was an unqualified success and he followed in the steps of two very different men, James Stewart and Patrick Buchan-Hepburn, who had been successful in their particular ways. He had few enemies despite the fact that he could be extremely tough. He was very close to Harold Macmillan who could have had no more loyal or efficient lieutenant. He is, I believe, the first Chief Whip to become Prime Minister.

Edward Heath was also the first leader of the Party to be elected by his colleagues in the House of Commons. Despite this he was subject to more attacks than any of those who had been imposed upon them. There may be a lesson to be learned from that, although I am certain that it is the right procedure.

When Heath was elected he was hailed as the very man the Party needed. Within weeks it was being said that his lower-middle-class background was a handicap and not an advantage as had been predicted, despite the fact that he was a Balliol man, an ex-President of the Oxford Union and a former Commanding Officer of one of the regiments of the Honourable Artillery Company. Then it was declared that it was inappropriate for the leader of the Conservative Party to be seen conducting carols : he should take an interest in popular and virile sports. When he won the Sydney to Hobart race the same people said that he should be at home looking after the political scene : in any case how could he afford it? After endless complaints that he should speak up it was asserted that his outline of policy at Selsdon Park was premature and would allow the Labour Party to pull it to pieces. At one point things reached such a pitch that it seemed possible that an attempt would be made to remove him from the leadership.

When Edward Heath became Prime Minister after a General Election campaign in which he played the major role the critics executed a hurried *volte-face*. They said they had always known that good old Ted would make it. Such is the world of politics. Time will provide the real answer, but it does not seem improbable that Edward Heath could prove to be the best leader and the best Prime Minister the Conservatives have had since Disraeli. Jo Grimond has said of him : 'He has a genuine integrity, a desire to do well for his country, and I think he likes administration . . . He has a very good collected mind. He gives it to subjects and is not easily distracted. He is also I think a courageous politician . . . Further, I think he's a fair man whom people would trust, and this is rather important in a party leader.' That is a fair assessment. I would merely add that he knows what he wants to do and he will do it and those who oppose him will find that they have a fight on their hands.

The most spectacular member of the 'Class of 1950' was Enoch Powell. Academically he was undoubtedly the most intelligent of a highly intelligent group. Much has been written by him and about him. To that I have nothing to add. He once insisted on my accompanying him up a hill at Llandudno in the dark while it was raining and a gale was blowing. He walked at great speed talking all the time. I can't remember a word he said because I couldn't hear and I was completely out of breath.

Enoch Powell is an individualist who believes in individualism. 'He thinks too much, such men are dangerous' is a reaction which occurs in the minds of many of his colleagues. He is a patriot without being a nationalist: he is a progressive Conservative who has faith in the traditions of the Party. Like his Cambridge predecessor Geoffrey Butler, the uncle of R.A.B., he thinks that 'the captains of Toryism in the past can be made the instructors of Toryism in the present'. But he tends to overlook the fact that the qualities of the instructor for battle and those of the leader in battle can differ.

It is a misfortune that he is not a member of the 1970 Conservative Government, particularly now that it has lost Ian Macleod. Edward Heath had no alternative but to dismiss him from the Shadow Cabinet after Powell had made a speech of a kind which clearly should have been passed by him first. To have ignored this breach would have been to undermine his own authority as leader, which was in question at the time, and to have weakened the conception of Cabinet responsibility, which must be applied just as much to the Shadow Cabinet if that organisation is to mean anything.

I believe that the Conservative Party is flexible enough for such a breach to be healed, particularly now the Party is in power. I hope that it will be, but it will be a matter of give and take on both sides. Powell said of the immigration issue: 'To see and not to speak would be the great betrayal.' That is a philosophy which is shared by both men and it should therefore be possible for the gap to be bridged. But what is possible is not always probable.

I was happy to move in such circles which were both entertaining and instructive. After the Blackpool Conference of 1958 I returned to Westminster fully recovered after my illness and ready for an exhilarating session. I was able to make my first real speech from the despatch box, as both Selwyn and David Ormsby-Gore were away. It went rather well and I even escaped attack from Aneurin Bevan. The following week I took part in quite a successful programme on Granada TV. I felt that I was really making progress. A week later it was all over.

4 How to fall off a Mountain

When you walk through a storm, hold your head up high
And don't be afraid of the dark.

OSCAR HAMMERSTEIN

I THINK it is reasonable to conclude that by the autumn of 1958 my political career was not going too badly. No one who has any real experience of politics is so foolish as to predict the future either generally or personally. As Harold Wilson said, 'A week is a long time in politics', and so for him in 1970 it proved to be. The road to the front bench is littered with men who were once considered to be future Prime Ministers and who fell by the wayside without even achieving junior office.

For some the way up the political mountain is easy, or comparatively so, for others it is hard. I am inclined to agree with my old friend John Carvel that for those who have to fight, the ultimate achievement is both more satisfying and more satisfactory. I was to deny myself all chance of that achievement. When such things happen it is little consolation to be able to say that one can blame only oneself.

Although I had been a homosexual all my life I had only once had any physical experience before the end of the war. This involved, as I have recorded, an older boy who had been specifically asked by his parents, who were friends of my stepfather, to look after me at Fettes. He certainly carried out his instructions in no uncertain manner, but hardly in the way they had envisaged. Although he was two years older than I was he was in the same form.

He was extremely tough: I relied on him to fight my battles and he relied on me to do his prep. As he lived in London it was a relationship which continued during the holidays and after he had left school when he joined the Regular Army, for which he was well suited. He was killed when the Nazi armies hurtled across France in 1940.

Despite this relationship, which I never regretted and I never thought to be wrong, I never had any similar associations again with anyone who was, as my mother would have described it, 'one of our class'. It was always, and still is, my firm belief that homosexuality is only an offence when a man uses his powers to seduce someone under his authority or who is a minor. I would never have permitted myself to indulge in this practice during my time in the Army. This may seem odd, as it is well known that uniforms have a peculiar attraction for the homosexual; moreover, conditions of war are liable to promote homosexual associations owing to the absence of women. I found this no particular deprivation. I can claim without conceit that the fact that I was a homosexual at heart made me more considerate towards the problems of the men who came under my control. There is nothing particularly unusual in that, nor is it harmful provided that the interest is properly controlled. Even so, it is unreasonable to expect that the desire should be entirely suppressed. I think that the effort of controlling that desire over six years contributed to what subsequently happened. I put it no higher than that.

When the war was over I went to live in a bed-sitting room in a house in Trevor Square which is near the Household Cavalry Barracks in Knightsbridge. I did not choose it for that reason. I noticed on my way home from dinner in the evenings that the troopers, who were in uniform, wandered up and down and then disappeared into the Park. At that time there were no railings, as these had been used for munitions during the war and it was impossible to lock up the area after midnight.

Finally, out of curiosity, I decided to go into the Park to see what went on. Under the darkness of the trees there was a veritable parade. I was intrigued. As I walked back to my digs I realised that a trooper was following me. I did not let him in, although I watched him through the window standing around expectantly. After about five minutes he went away disappointed to search, no doubt, for someone more co-operative. I was on the brink.

About a fortnight later I was returning from a dinner party where the wine had flowed freely. I thought I would get some fresh air before turning in. I sat down on a seat and a trooper came and sat down next to me. He was a Scots boy who came from Edinburgh and we got into conversation about Scotland and his life in the Army. Neither of us had any illusions about the ultimate purpose of our conversation, and this was duly achieved. I never saw him again.

The next morning I was in a state of mental panic. What was more surprising and even ridiculous, in view of the very moderate activity which had taken place, was that I was in a cold sweat in case I had contracted some disease. All of which goes to show how remarkably immature I was despite my experience of life and the fact that I was then thirty-one. After a month had passed I decided that I had not become infected in any way and having enjoyed my first experience I decided to try it again. So began the road to disaster which I continued to pursue, off and on, for thirteen years. Along that road I made a number of contacts, some of them temporary 'steadies'. Although I got to know some of them quite well and looked forward to meeting them again I never took any of them with me in public. I discovered a very convenient place near the Peter Pan statue in Kensington Gardens. J. M. Barrie, unlike some of his successors, would hardly have approved. Peter Pan had his back to us so I could not be accused of polluting the young.

In view of my undoubted political ambitions, this conduct could well be adjudged as verging on insanity. Every time it was over I pretended to myself that this was definitely the last time. I knew perfectly well the risk I was running and exactly what would happen if I were caught. Although alcohol stimulated my desire and often eliminated any power I might have to resist temptation, I was never in such a state that I did not know what I was doing. Oscar Wilde said, in the same context, 'It was like feasting with panthers: the danger was half the excitement.' I cannot pretend that the danger had the same effect upon me. In fact it had the reverse. I was lucky in that only on one occasion was there any attempt at violence and that was when I became involved with someone who was not in the Armed Forces. I usually took care never to carry a wallet or any marks of identification on me or any money in excess of what was required for the purpose. From a state of immaturity I became highly professional.

In the early days a quite absurd case of a much more moderate nature occurred which should have certainly shown me the red light. William Field, a Labour M.P., was had up for soliciting sailors in public in London. He was found guilty and as a result had to resign his seat in Parliament which was a heavy price to pay for a wink and a smile. At the Carlton Club where I was lunching on the day of his conviction there were lewd suggestions that this was just what one would expect of Labour M.P.s and that the only surprising thing was that more of them had not been caught.

Oddly enough I knew Field, as his mother had been my grandfather's housekeeper for many years. He was a very presentable and likable person of whom even my stepfather approved, although he could not understand how it was that he was both a Catholic and a Socialist. But then my stepfather was not only a right-wing Conservative but also a right-wing Catholic.

At that time the question of Homosexual Law Reform was not a political issue of any magnitude. Had it been I have no doubt that the Labour Government might well have considered that all homosexuals should be nationalised. Had I had any doubt on the subject the reaction to the Field case at the Carlton Club would have convinced me. What made the case even more ridiculous was that Field had not made any progress with his advances: a stiff warning would surely have met the case from everyone's point of view. The suggestion made in Conservative quarters that his action was calculated to undermine the morale of His Majesty's Forces was, in my opinion, highly laughable. I got myself into serious trouble with a former friend and colleague, Harry Legge-Bourke, now chairman of the 'all-powerful 1922 Committee' and who had been in 'the Blues', by asking him if it was true that the troopers had to pay five per cent of their earnings into the regimental funds. I thought he would never speak to me again. He had just produced an illustrated book on life in the Household Cavalry in which, needless to say, there was no reference to that part of their activities.

Not all Conservative M.P.s subscribed to the view that homosexuality was 'that abominable crime not to be mentioned among Christians'. I remember the occasion when one of them recounted that he had been sent a letter by some of his homosexual constituents, which was in itself courageous, asking him what he was prepared to do about the law on the subject and what was his own opinion in the matter. To this he adroitly replied, '*Chacun à son trou.*' It was perhaps just as well that the seat was subsequently abolished. He told this story in the sacred precincts of the Carlton Club where it was received with extremely modified rapture. Not only should it not have been mentioned among Christians, but also certainly not among gentlemen.

At a later stage in this story I shall examine what was said in the House of Commons during the passage of the Sexual Offences Bill in 1967. The year of my downfall was 1958. A year before that the Wolfenden Report on Homosexual Offences and Prostitution had appeared. The fact that it took ten years for anything to be done about the recommendations contained in Part II, which was concerned with homosexuality, indicates the reaction of the Conservative Government, which was in power most of that time, to the whole subject. I was clearly on dangerous ground and I knew it. If anything were to happen to me I could expect no sympathy from those with whom I was most closely associated, and I knew that too. I record this in case it should be thought by anyone who reads this book that the treatment I received was not justified or that I resented it. As I have noted, it is common practice in our present society to break the ten commandments with comparative impunity, but it is not permissible to break the eleventh. This I did and paid the price.

The occasion of my doing so was on a dark and misty November night. I had been to a dinner at the Polish Embassy. I had accepted the invitation against my will as it was a Wednesday and it was my normal practice to be in Harrow on Wednesday evenings to deal with the problems of my constituents. As a result I found myself dealing with a somewhat greater problem of my own. It was a pleasant occasion and there was a good deal to drink. But I was not drunk, although it was subsequently suggested that I should have said I was as an extenuating circumstance. I considered this suggestion neither valid nor dignified.

I went back to the House for a division which never took place and then I left for the last time, although I was not to know that. As it was not a cold night and as I felt in need of some fresh air I parked the car near Storey's Gate and went into St. James's Park. It was just after eleven o'clock and the guardsmen were returning to Wellington Barracks as the pubs were emptying. I had decided

D*

to make a circle of the Park and I was walking down the Mall which admittedly is a known place for homosexual pick-ups. A young guardsman in uniform passed me at a slow pace and I knew what that meant. I turned and caught up with him and we went together into the Park.

Had I been more alert I would have known from past experience that the place where we went was regularly patrolled before midnight. The good dinner plus a liberal quantity of Kirsch had, however, dulled my senses. As a result we were caught by a park official accompanied by a policeman. Then began the terrible journey back to Cannon Row police station. In a moment of wild insanity I decided to try to make a break for it. The result was a short sharp struggle where the result was never in doubt.

On arrival at Cannon Row I pretended at first that I was somebody else and gave a false name, but then I realised how foolish that was, as I was bound to be recognised. When I disclosed my true identity there was a certain amount of consternation. The officer in charge of the police at the House of Commons was sent for. He was a man with whom I had always been on very good terms, as indeed I was with all the police in the establishment, who have a difficult job to do and do it extremely well. Meanwhile I had been put in a cell for the first time in my life.

At 3.30 a.m. I was allowed to go free on the understanding that I would appear at Bow Street at 10.00 a.m. I walked back to my car and drove back to Richmond. Alone in the darkness with the mist coming in patches outside I began to realise what lay ahead. It is not an hour at which anyone is at their best even under normal conditions. In the past I had often thought of what I would do if such a misfortune were to happen. I envisaged that I would drive to the coast to Beachy Head and go full-tilt over the top : that would have been a dramatic finale. Now it had happened I had no such intention. It was not because I was afraid : in many ways it would have been a much less alarming experience than that which faced me. I knew then, as I have known ever since, that a man cannot run away and remain a man, and that suicide, although it requires courage, is a coward's way out.

I got home at about 4.00 a.m. and slept until seven o'clock. How I managed to do that I do not know. I suppose it was sheer mental exhaustion and nature kindly intervened knowing that I would require all my strength. I even managed to eat breakfast with the family, although I found it difficult to explain the marks under my eyes which were the result of my struggle with the law. Then I drove to London and left my car outside the Foreign Office, as I would normally have done if I had been going to begin the day's work. I walked along the Embankment and at 9.45 a.m. presented myself at Bow Street. My case was taken first and was merely a formality, as it had been decided to defer proceedings for further consideration by both the police and myself. The Press was there in force, but at that stage the public were unaware of what had happened. The police were kindness itself and arranged for me to be driven away in one of their own cars to the Foreign Office. There I went immediately to see Selwyn and tendered my resignation which was not accepted for the time being. I then drove home.

At that point I began to feel dazed and sick. My doctor was sent for and gave me a sedative. Around lunchtime Quintin Hogg came and we discussed what action to take and I told him the whole story, although by that time the news had broken. I then went to bed and my brother-in-law, Christopher Mayhew, came to be with us. The evening papers made headlines of the event, but I was not allowed to see them. In any case I was by then in a drugged stupor. Then followed the telephone calls from kind friends and next day a spate of letters, most of them sympathetic but some of them offensive. I read them all and replied to some.

The next morning I went to see a firm of solicitors who were judged to be best qualified to deal with this type of case. The trial was set for December 10th, which meant that there was a delay of three weeks, and my wife and I decided that it would be best to leave home for part of the time. We had seats for the theatre on the Friday night and we decided to go. It was the theatre production of *Auntie Mame*, a book which had made me laugh a great deal. Despite everything I even managed to laugh at the play.

When I returned from the country my solicitor and I went to see the barrister whom they had decided to brief. This was John Laurence, who was afterwards to become a judge and died at an early age. It had been agreed that I should plead guilty and thus enable me to resign my seat. It also meant that the case would be over and done with, one way or the other, in a single day and there would be no protracted proceedings at the Old Bailey with all the accompanying publicity. So far as I was concerned the main damage was done and there was no good purpose to be served for anyone by adding to it.

I therefore tendered my resignation from office and from the House of Commons and was duly appointed Steward of the Manor of Northstead.

When I informed the Chairman of Harrow East, Theo Constantine, of my decision he urged me to reconsider it. The constituency Association, ever loyal, were prepared to stand by me. I appreciated this more than I can say. But I knew that there were many people who, whilst they were my supporters, regarded what I had done as unspeakable. It would have been straining their loyalty to the Party too far to have remained. I knew, as one who had a very practical knowledge of the ways of the Press, that there would be a violent outcry in certain quarters which would damage the Party in Harrow East and lead to the very kind of internal dissension which I had always striven to avoid. As it was, John Gordon, that patriarchal Scottish moralist, was kind enough to say when it was all over that although he had never met me, which was not true, he believed I had behaved correctly in departing. That was a commendation which should stand me in good stead at the last judgement.

Sydney Silverman, who was the last person with whom I had crossed swords at question time, wrote: 'Stick to your guns.' It was a kindly gesture from an opponent. I replied, 'No guns to stick to.' He, on a much more important issue, stuck to his and was deservedly successful.

The day before the case it was the Oxford and Cambridge rugby match at Twickenham which I always attended and at which I always met many friends. I decided to go. I can't say it was the match that I most enjoyed, although Oxford won. Several of my ex-colleagues, as I now had to regard them, from the House of Commons were there. They obviously did not know whether to wish me luck or to say good-bye. So they solved the problem by not saying anything. They were all well-trained politicians and good Conservatives.

The case took place at Bow Street on the morning of December 10th. I walked there with my solicitor, a most calm and helpful man, who was optimistic as to the result and told my wife to expect us back at his office within the hour. There was apparently no reserved seat for me in the 'black maria', after all. Whenever I see one on its way from the courts now I feel the greatest sympathy for the inmates, whatever they may have done.

Laurence spoke on my behalf in mitigation. It was a well delivered speech which we had discussed together. In fact I can claim to have made a number of suggestions. I was still qualified to do that. I remember his saying, 'He will pay for this for the rest of his life.' How right he was. Then I stood in the dock with the guardsman standing stiffly to attention beside me. The courtroom was jam-packed, and the Press, many of whom I knew, were there *en masse*. I was fined five pounds for breaking the park regulations. So was the guardsman and I paid his fine as well. I felt it was the least I could do.

I went out into Covent Garden with my solicitor. He wanted to catch a taxi, although his office was only five minutes away. But we were immediately surrounded by the Press and the photographers and I knew that they had their job to do. I said I would talk to them and let them take their photographs and suggested that he should go on, which he did, saying kindly that he admired my courage. It was not in fact courage, as I knew that if I got it all over there and then I was less likely to be plagued with demands for interviews on the telephone. And so it turned out. One of the photographers nearly had his camera smashed by an angry woman who shouted, 'Leave the poor devil alone.' I stood on the corner for about ten minutes answering questions and being photographed. I felt no resentment because I knew that they were only doing their job and I wanted to make it as easy for them as I could. One or two of the Covent Garden porters had some uncomplimentary remarks to make, but they were not all that serious about it. On the whole the proceedings passed off quite well and my wife drove me home.

That afternoon we had a party for my second daughter's birthday. A number of her friends came and we all played games and ate birthday cake. At the end their parents came to collect them and I received them, and they spoke to me as if nothing had happened. When they had all gone I had two double Scotches and took an extra sleeping pill. It was the beginning of a bad habit which was to take me years to break.

The next day I went to see Harold Macmillan at 10 Downing Street. He was very kind and sympathetic. Tony Barber then let me out of the back garden gate. I took leave of my Foreign Office staff when I went to pay my respects to my successor Jack Profumo. For him too there were rough days ahead. The nicest thing that was said was by one of my women P.A.s who remarked sadly 'Oh dear, now we shall all have to be polite again.' That made me feel better. I needed some encouragement, as I felt that my powers of endurance were beginning to run out and it was not the time for that to happen.

I felt that it would be right to tender my resignation from all the clubs to which I belonged. The Carlton Club, to which I had belonged for twenty-two years, accepted it without comment. The Junior Carlton Club wrote to say that in view of my political services to the Club they hoped I would retain my membership, but they asked me to give an undertaking that I would not go into the Club for two years. I thought this was rather an expensive indignity, so I declined to give the assurance and resigned. The Chairman of Pratt's, which was far the most select of them all, wrote a charming note saying that he did not think it was necessary for me to go and urged me not to do so. I knew, however, that there were a number of members who were less broad-minded who would have objected to my appearing there.

I was told later that the War Office had proposed that I should be cashiered. As I had had nothing to do with the Territorial Army, in which I held the rank of lieutenant-colonel, for seven years this was just vindictive. Had I been involved with a sailor or an airman I doubt if they would have considered the matter. Fortunately my friend Hugh Fraser, who was Under-Secretary of State, intervened and stopped them. I am surprised that they did not suggest a special parade at which, like another artillery officer, Dreyfus, I would have all my badges of rank torn off and my medals taken away. This would have been a slightly excessive punishment for breaking park regulations. As I have never since been invited to any ceremony at which it would be required to wear decorations I would not have been embarrassed by their loss. I have, in fact, now lost them.

Most of my friends were kind, although only a few went out of their way to seek me out. I quite understood their position and I did not seek them out. When a man is deeply involved in politics, as I was, his private life is diminished and he has few personal friends outside the political circle. Many that he had before entering politics take it as a slight that he does not see them more often drop him. I found myself largely isolated, which was not a great help, as it was bound to make me introspective. Whereas in the past there was hardly a day when I was not involved in addressing a meeting, speaking at a lunch or dinner, attending receptions and parties, now no further invitations arrived. I can count the number I have received since 1958 on the fingers of both hands. For a gregarious person this was a punishing experience. What depressed me most was that my days of public speaking were over. I had always found this exhilarating and in many ways this was the worst of my deprivations. For those who had to listen to me this may have come as a happy release, but for me it was almost unendurable. Up to then I had always kept a diary. As there was nothing of interest to write in it I closed it with the words 'The rest is silence'. I was becoming slightly melodramatic. What was worse, I was bored to death. Unfortunately when you are bored to death you don't die, at least not physically. I once said of a colleague that he was the greatest living exponent of life after death. I suddenly found that I had taken over his title.

One of the things that worried me most was that as a result of what I had done Harrow East would once again fall into the hands of the enemy. I need not have worried. My successor, who was not a man of great political distinction, got as large a majority at the by-election as I had done in 1955. When he subsequently lost the seat, which he should never have done, I was very depressed, as, without being conceited, I knew that I could have held it. Others who had won similar seats in 1950 held theirs and have today even doubled or trebled their majorities. It was therefore a great relief to me that the seat was won back in 1970. It was ten years before I could summon up the courage to go back into the constituency, and then only to a private lunch with friends.

The Conservative Party, quite understandably because of its outlook and make-up, did not want to know anything more about me. Even when they were in trouble they did not ask for my views on the issues of propaganda, although I was qualified to give them and would willingly have done so without charge. I do not resent this because I understand my party better than most and for that reason, amongst others, it is still my party.

Dingle Foot, whom I only knew slightly as a result of talking to him prior to my visit to Ghana and because he was Michael's brother and an ex-President of the Oxford Union, gave a cocktail party for me to which a number of Labour M.P.s came. The Labour Party has always treated me with great consideration and kindness which I have greatly appreciated. Admittedly I had never been personally hostile to any of them in the House of Commons because I believed most of them to be sincere in their beliefs. It was only on matters of practice that we fundamentally disagreed. It has been cynically remarked that in the House of Commons it is only on one's own side that one has real enemies: when you are on the front bench they are well placed to stab you in the back. Despite my experiences I have never gone so far as to subscribe to this although I have had my moments of doubt.

As an Anglo-Catholic I naturally turned to the Church in my moment of difficulty; but I may say that the Church made no attempt to turn to me. My local vicar, who had written to me some months before to ask if I could see my way to suggest his promotion in the appropriate quarters, received me somewhat coldly. He clearly still held to the view 'inter Christianis non nominandum'. But the purpose of my visit was to mention it. His immediate question was to ask whether I had been to confession before taking communion at midnight mass on Christmas Day. I replied that I had done so at All Saints Church, Margaret Street, where I often attended, and had done so for nearly thirty years. I asked him why he wanted to know and he said that he had been asked by a number of his congregation who felt that anyone who had been involved in 'a national scandal', as he put it, should not have done so. I terminated the interview at once and never went into his church again. I then went to see the Vicar of All Saints, the Rev. Kenneth Ross, who had been pleased to have an M.P. amongst his congregation, which also included Harold Macmillan's brother, who always wore a top hat. Father Ross had written a pamphlet entitled 'Letter to a Homosexual' but he had never written to me. I had read the pamphlet, which was priced ninepence, and without being unkind it was expensive at the price. My interview with him was equally valueless. I had one further interview with a young priest who was so ignorant about the whole subject that I ended up by explaining it all to him in words of one syllable. I left him almost speechless and red in the face, which, at least, had its funny side. For me the Anglo-Catholics were on the way out; but I was not at all certain who was on the way in, although I had a shrewd idea.

In the early days of 1959 I had to set about finding something to do and this was not easy. Two courses lay open to me. Either I could go back to my old occupation of advertising or I could start afresh in something quite different. My old firm, W. S. Crawford Ltd., were not prepared to take me back, despite a letter I had received from the Chairman when the storm had broken saying that the doors were open. I think he had assumed that I would be sent to prison and that he would have the benefit of having made a Christian gesture without having to carry it out. Possibly he was overruled by his colleagues who felt it would be bad for the business. I was not really qualified to take up any other work and was in any case too well known; the barriers were up against me.

One of my colleagues who was in the advertising business was reported as saying 'The only thing for Ian Harvey to do is to change his name and go to Canada.' I doubt very much if the Canadian authorities would have welcomed this proposal. A few months later he failed signally as a junior Minister and was returned to the back benches. I was tempted to send him a telegram saying: 'Change your name and go to Canada.' But I decided that the gibe was too cheap to merit the cost of a telegram. The Conservative Party took the view that a political muddle was not in the same category as a social misdemeanour and gave him a baronetcy.

Arthur Varley, Chairman of Colman, Prentis and Varley, came to my rescue and gave me an assignment. At a later date he disclosed to me that he had done so largely because his agency handled the Conservative Party advertising account and Oliver Poole, the Chairman, had already had a word in his ear. The nature of my assignment was not exactly clear. I was given an office in Jermyn Street which was somewhat humorous, in view of its former reputation. The office was in the centre of the building and had no windows. I had no secretary and not even a typewriter. I was not allowed to see any clients and the fact that I was there was kept a dark secret. Although I was grateful, it was not exactly the best way in which to begin the task of rehabilitation.

It was not surprising that the tide of depression began to flow in upon me: and depression is a dangerous mental condition. I decided that I would consult a psychiatrist, although all I had heard made me suspect them of being slightly more in need of attention than their clients. I have not entirely reversed that opinion. I felt, and still feel, that unloading one's troubles on one's friends is an unwarranted liberty. I knew that my problems were of such a nature that unless I lost complete mental self-control there was little anyone else could do about them. The last thing I wanted was sympathy. On the other hand, one could demand assistance if one paid for it. Whether or not one got it was quite another matter.

It would not be fair, and I suspect it would be unprofessional, if I were to disclose the name of the man I went to see. His consulting room was at the best address. He was an excessively dull man and gave the impression of wearing a mask so that he appeared not to react to anything I said. If this was an act it was a very good one, but I had a sneaking suspicion that he always looked like that. I refused point blank to lie on his couch, as I have never thought it necessary to be prostrate in order to conduct an intelligent conversation. No doubt some of the conversations he conducted were not intelligent and he probably thought mine was not either. We went through all the rigmarole and I could see him making notes on such subjects as 'Oedipus complex', heredity, marital conditions and, probably, paranoia. I got the impression that he was groping more than probing. He was clearly disappointed that I was neither on the verge of insanity nor desperately anxious to be cured of this terrible disease. If either had been the case he had a course clearly mapped out. As it was he was confronted with a new situation and he was not helped by the fact that as we went along I both cross-examined and contradicted him. Quite clearly the best clients did not do that sort of thing. I was obviously not co-operative and co-operation, he pointed out, was the basis of success.

Just as I had decided that this was an expensive and unproductive relationship he announced that he thought he had come up with a winner. An American colleague had produced a new tranquilliser which had proved successful in dealing with the most complex cases. He thought I should try it. I was ready to try anything so I agreed. He gave me some pills which were extremely expensive and told me to take five a day: one on waking, one midmorning, one after lunch, one in the evening and one before going to bed. After two days of this I was to come and discuss the results with him. By the time I had taken the second pill I was feeling decidedly sleepy. I took the third and a few moments later fell under my desk unconscious. So ended my first adventures in the psychiatric field. At a later date I was persuaded to try hypnosis. This was an uproarious experience. At the point when I was assured by my mentor, if that is the right word, that I was in such a state of subjection that I could not lift my legs, I reacted smartly by performing a physical exercise which quite surprised me and infuriated him. I was once again accused of not co-operating.

At a later date, when alcohol and mental strain had taken their toll, a far more intelligent man to whom I committed myself said that I had tried to fight my battle by myself and that this should never have been allowed to happen. I suppose he was right but with due respect to him I do not see, looking back, that anyone else was either competent or prepared to help. That was partly due to my own arrogance which was remarkably unaffected and partly due to the fact that I erected a façade which successfully convinced a number of people that I did not need help. What went on behind it got increasingly out of control and eventually it cracked.

As my family were distillers I suppose it is reasonable to deduce that I had alcohol in my blood. One of my great-uncles was exiled by the family to the Isle of Arran because he regularly held up the trams in Glasgow on Saturday nights by lying on the rails and then giving the name of the local minister as a reference when he was taken to the police station. In relating this I suppose I am lending support to all those who condemn the evils of drink. As with all things it is, in my opinion, a question of excess and what is exsessive for some is not excessive for others. It has been said that once an alcoholic always an alcoholic. I believe this to be non-sense, although once the border line has been passed the farther one goes the more difficult it is to get back. It is also a matter of circumstances. For the man who is in trouble and depressed it is a way out. The fact that it is not the right way out is likely to be irrelevant to him until disaster hits so hard that either he brings it to a halt or gives up hope and is carried away on the flood.

The advertising fraternity had a bad reputation in the past for being littered with alcoholics and in the days when advertising campaigns were sold under the influence of dry martinis this was partly true. On the other hand there have been many advertising men of my acquaintance who were far more interesting, and on occasions more creative, when they were drunk than when they were sober. One of them for whom I had both a high regard and affection produced his best work when slightly inebriated and it was a lot better than that of some of his colleagues who kept to tomato juice. Two of my superiors in the early days who detested

one another underwent a strange conversion. The one, whom I
spent many hours extricating from some extremely low dives in
the Strand, died teetotal. The other who was always denouncing
him for his alcoholic habits and never touched a drop before sun-
down ended up in an alcoholic stupor. I went to both their memorial services and was intrigued by the delicacy of the tributes paid
to them.

In many ways it was foolish of me to go back into advertising
which is an occupation fraught with stresses and strains, of which
I had already had quite enough. But I had little alternative. I realised that I might run into trouble and I did. But trouble had become for me only a comparative experience.

I had to face up to the problems of a major readjustment at a
particularly difficult time, not only in my own life but also in the
development of society as a whole. Had it all happened ten years
later circumstances might have been very different on both counts,
and I shall have more to say about this when I examine these de-
velopments in more detail. Over a period of thirteen years I had
to face the fact that my public and private lives were a contra-
diction in terms. It was a schizophrenic existence and schizophrenia
in any circumstances is liable to defeat both diagnosis and cure.
I do not claim that this was in any way an original condition peculiar to me, but it was a condition which was made more complex
by the position I held. So long as I successfully achieved a balance
I was in company with many people, some of whom I knew. Once
I failed I created a place for myself which has been occupied by
comparatively few. That is the only reason why I think it is of
interest to anyone else to place my experiences on record.

I have already set down my views on the proper responsibilities
of public life in a democracy. In my reaction to what I did and to
what happened to me I was firmly guided by these responsibilities,
and on that score at least I think I behaved properly. It is not a
happy course to have to take, but I am bound to recommend it to
anyone who should find himself in a similar predicament, even
with the changes in public opinion. It is after all a field in which
I can claim to have certain qualifications.

As I have indicated the House of Commons is peculiarly attractive to those who become members. One of my colleagues once
described it as being a ringside seat on life and there is great truth
in that. Many of those who lose their seats wander about discon-

solately and cannot wait to get back. When one thinks of the all-night sittings and the hours of boredom during committee stages when one is not taking part but has to vote, it is quite surprising that this should be so. It has been described as a club, but it is far more than that because of its inherent sense of responsibility for the lives of those outside. There are of course those for whom it has no such attraction and in due course they make their exits, leaving nothing behind them and taking nothing with them, except perhaps a title which they do not really deserve. Despite the continuous attacks on M.P.s and denunciations from all quarters, many of them unqualified and ill-informed, that the repute of Parliament has never been so low, it is a position which still commands attention and ultimately respect.

Having worked to achieve all this and then to shatter it in a single unguarded hour was a heavy blow to me. Despite kindly assurances from numerous well-intentioned but misguided people that I would be back once it had all blown over, I knew that this was completely untrue. The gates were closed to me for ever and I could only remain on the outside looking in which is a terrible experience for one who has been on the inside looking out. Psychologically it carried with it the most damaging and dangerous of all conditions – deprivation. It was little consolation to be told that public memory is short and it will all soon be forgotten. That may be a truism but it is not a personal truth.

One of the most difficult aspects of readjustment for me was the fact that I had gone too far and seen too much. I had gone far enough up the mountain to know what it looked like at the top. As Laurence had pointed out at Bow Street, I had to become used to the comparative obscurity of private life, and I was not cut out for it. Men whom I used to meet daily were now on a different plane and I was forced to watch their progress in the public eye and to know that I might have achieved the same heights. Whether this would have in fact happened neither I nor anyone else will ever know. That in itself is a source of continuous and nagging aggravation : it creates a world of might-have-been which, in some respects, is more difficult to live in than the world which is.

A young man who was an accomplished equestrian and who lived for his horses once asked me at a dinner party if I missed political life. I replied that I felt the same as he would if he lost both his legs. I am glad to say that he had the good sense not to pursue the matter. Even more tiresome are those who say to me, 'Aren't you glad you're away from it all now?' Some people have very odd topics of conversation. There are, of course, many who have succeeded in rising above physical and social handicaps. I have nothing but admiration for them. I do not claim to have had such success and I make no excuse by claiming that the barriers erected in my path are too high. I am just not as good a climber as I used to be.

Probably one of the most refined forms of torture that was invented for me was in the shape of dreams. I have on many occasions dreamed that I was back exactly where I was and that nothing had happened. I have then woken up to the unpleasant realisation that things are not what they used to be. I feel sure that Jung would have been intrigued by it but personally I can do without it.

On returning to advertising I was once more in a society which was quite different from that of politics. When I had first started, with the intention of linking the one up with the other, I had regarded it as a means to an end, and it proved to be very successful but it had now become the end itself, at least for the time being. Without being unkind or unduly conceited, I had to regard my intellectual inferiors as my superiors. I have no doubt that some of them knew it and tended to take advantage of it. I will not deny that this was a situation which invoked cynicism on my part and on occasions drove me to drink: and there was plenty of drink about.

Peter Wildeblood in his remarkable account of his experiences during the Montagu trial and afterwards in prison, a courageous personal testament about which I shall have more to say, makes some observations on the subject of marriage. He writes: 'I think it is more honest and less harmful for a man with homosexual tendencies to recognise himself for what he is. He will always be lonely: he must accept that. He will never enjoy the companionship that comes with marriage or the joy of watching his children grow up, but he will at least have the austere consolation of self-knowledge and integrity.'

In principle there is very little I can fault in that statement. But being young Peter Wildeblood tended to fall into the trap of generalisation, or more accurately of applying the particular to the general, which has bedevilled all arguments on the subject of homosexuality. I was never under the mistaken impression that

I could change with marriage, but I took the view that the acceptance of what is regarded as a normal condition of life would help
control abnormal tendencies. To an extent I was proved right.

Admittedly I had very serious reservations about marriage for
very much the same reasons that Wildeblood gives. I had determined not to get married during the war because I had the example
of my father before me and, as I have said, I felt it the height of
folly to risk leaving a mother and family without a father as my
mother and I were left. Moreover in total war they would have been
liable to meet as much danger as I was. But I had always contem-
plated marriage for when it was over. I had seen the elderly bache-
lors sitting alone and dejected in the evenings at my various clubs
and had decided that it was not the end for me. I knew that politically it was both helpful and desirable to be married. I also wanted
a family and in particular a son.

The two factors which I omitted from my calculations were
love and sex or, to be more exact, I did not calculate them properly. Having observed the results of numerous marriages in
which both played a major part at the outset, this failure on my
part was perhaps not so grotesque as it may seem at first sight.
When I got married I had never had sex with a woman nor had
I ever desired to have it. For me it was the act necessary to the
procreation of children according to the instructions of the Church.
So far as I was concerned companionship was my interpretation of
love. I will accept Wildeblood's implied censure that I was lacking
in integrity and, to an extent, in self-knowledge.

I have never thought that my craving for a son had any basic
association with my homosexuality. Henry VIII, who had a similar
obsession, could by no stretch of the imagination be regarded as
anything but an extreme heterosexual. I think it is a normal characteristic in many men that they want to hand on the future to
their sons and in a sense live their lives again through them. This
has had on many occasions disastrous results. The intelligent parent
is the one who provides the right conditions in which the children
can grow up and knows when the time has come to step aside and
let them live their own lives.

It is one of the most disturbing features of our time that the
generation gap, about which, admittedly, a great deal of nonsense
is written, is in fact a reality. For this, parents must be held
primarily responsible, not only because of the way in which they

treat their children, but also because of the way in which they behave in front of them. When I was at school it was quite unusual for the parents of any boy to be divorced, and the matter was never discussed with him. Today it seems to be almost an anomaly for them to live together. The so-called progressive members of society who regard marriage as an out-dated ritual would do well to note the damage that has been done to the future generation, of whom so many suffer from a lack of security.

Nor can the educationalists be absolved from blame, although their task is often complicated by parents whose way of life contradicts much of what children are taught at school. The teaching profession as a whole is so overworked and underpaid that a close study of individual children and the maintenance of good parent–teacher relationships are points which are only too often omitted from the curriculum. And these are serious omissions.

These facts were brought home to me when, as a Member of Parliament, I was closely involved with the schools in my constituency and with the problems of many parents. I promised myself that when my own children arrived I would take care to avoid the mistakes that had come to my notice. I do not think I entirely failed in this, and I was greatly assisted by my wife whose views were similar to my own, and by the fact that my children were normal and balanced. I was particularly concerned, not only because of my own experience, but also because of the cases of the often bad relationships between fathers and sons that came to my notice; this I determined should never happen to my son and myself.

As things transpired it did not arise: my first child was a girl and so was my second.

However, as one of my uncles had had nine daughters my wife and I thought it was time to call it a day. My son, therefore, never arrived. It would be a foolish flight of the imagination to believe that had he done so it would have changed me. The most that I can claim is that it might have helped me to stabilise my normal relationships with society through the determination to hand over a future intact to my heir. But that can justly be regarded as wishful thinking in the light of the powerful influence of my abnormal sexual impulses over my proper sense of responsibility.

I have embarked on this diversion because it will underline the impact of my personal disaster upon my family life, together with the resultant tide of guilt-complex which so far as my homosexuality *per se* was concerned had never before existed. This too made a considerable contribution to the stresses and strains with which I had to contend in these dark days. I had immediately offered my wife her freedom after the event and we had had to seriously consider whether it was in the best interests of the children for us to part or to stay together. Her loyalty to me at this time was beyond all bounds. The fact that she was in no way responsible made my burden of guilt even heavier. I have always had the most utter contempt for those people who bring children into the world and then run away from their responsibilities. It can also be argued that a man with my responsibilities who did what I did deserves equal contempt and I accept this. In our particular case the children were fortunately too young to know what had happened and those with whom they mixed were not capable of reading the papers. Provided we could maintain the semblance of happily married life in front of the children my wife and I decided that we should stay together, and I think we were right. The credit for this is hers and not mine. Looking back I do not think that we failed and that is some consolation.

Although in due course I was able to restore to a considerable degree my interest in life through my activities in advertising, and although I made many new friends who were both congenial and understanding, it was more like existing than living. The sense of frustration and of deprivation kept on returning like a bad attack of migraine. My mind went back to my Oxford days when my creative instincts alternated between Drury Lane and Westminster. So I began to write again but my whole system had been so jolted that my inspiration faltered. Critics may well say that it continues to do so, but at least it has occupied my mind and given me something to do which seemed worthwhile. I quickly discovered, although I suppose I knew it already, that whatever an M.P. writes, however trivial or badly expressed, it is sure of publication. The point is proved by a daily reading of the Press, particularly the letters to the editor, whereas the freelance contributor without a name is usually destined for the limbo or the returned MS with the rejection slip.

Despite the violence of my experience I remained sexually unchanged. The psychiatrist whom I consulted, and from whom I received little assistance apart from making me unconscious, suggested that I should try to find someone of my own class which would enable me to avoid the risks of my previous activities. In principle this was sound advice but in practice it was unrelated to my natural inclinations and make-up which he, as a psychiatrist, should have realised. This situation was not improved by the fact that I was now relatively unoccupied and mentally underemployed. I was virtually an exile from the society to which I had become accustomed. It seemed that my life had ended at forty-three: an age when most people are coming to a time of fruition. Instead of ripening, the apple, for me, had fallen off the tree and was mouldering on the grass and was fit only for the birds. I was living with dead dreams which created an atmosphere of spiritual depression and contained all the seeds of self-destruction. I was continually hankering after things which were no longer in my power to achieve.

When I had first entered advertising I had always planned to spend a period on the other side. That is to say I intended to switch from the advertising agency to the client who produced the goods which were advertised. The war interfered with this programme and afterwards, although I received a number of offers, I rejected them because it was not possible to combine them with a political career, as life in an agency had permitted. At least that was my opinion and the more reputable manufacturers agreed with me. There are a number of M.P.s on company boards and having seen them in action in the House of Commons I cannot believe that they can make any really constructive contribution to their companies' affairs. Their appointments are of dubious prestige value. It was not the sort of position I was prepared to accept and in any case I was only a prospective Parliamentary candidate in those early days.

When I no longer had a political career this objection ceased to exist. Consequently I accepted an invitation from one of my clients at Colman Prentis and Varley to join them. By this time I had restored my position in dealing with clients and become a director of the agency. My decision to cross the fence from agency to client was a grave mistake. The firm to which I went had an international reputation but it was a family business and was content to rest upon the laurels won by an older generation. Their successors did not possess the same acumen. They were all extremely rich men and they did not understand the problems of those who had to work to earn enough money to make ends meet. My first proposal to increase the wages of all the members of my underpaid department was regarded as the typical extravagance of an advertising man. They were all ultra-conservative and objected to change on principle. The Board was sterile and anyone who was not a member of the family had no real say in the conduct of affairs. The company was littered with relations who were being groomed for stardom over the heads of men of far greater ability. It was in every department the justification for the rise of Socialism in industry. For me it was an unhappy relationship which could not last. To misquote Oscar Wilde, it was like feasting with morons. It was not surprising that this experience increased my condition of frustration and depression to breaking point.

As a result I had to turn once again to the psychiatrists although up till then they had been of little help. But the new situation, although worse for me, was easier for them because my powers of resistance and self-assurance had broken down. This time I was more fortunate and found a man of intelligence who had a clear understanding of the problem and knew what had to be done to avert a major crisis, although in all conscience things were already bad enough. I had by then reached the level of not caring about which stage is the one before the point of no return.

The sanatorium to which I retreated as a result is one of the ugliest buildings in the country. If it had had 'abandon hope all ye who enter here' written over the gates I should not have been surprised. So far as I was concerned the reverse was to prove the case. I believe that the visitors book, which for obvious reasons is not open to public inspection, contains some extremely illustrious and well-known names. The clientele was extremely mixed and of both, and indeed mixed, sexes. The élite had rooms to themselves but the rest of us lived in dormitories which of course were male and female. We all ate together and the food was remarkably good. There was a games room and a television room where there was apt to be an argument from time to time over which programme should be watched. At night most people had sleeping pills so there was comparative quiet. At the back of the building there was a somewhat sinister block which contained patients who were not considered sufficiently under control to mix with the others. Every now and then one of our colleagues would disappear, either temporarily or permanently, as a result of some unfortunate lapse such as sticking his knife into his neighbour at the breakfast table.

There were men and woman there who had in their time played active and valuable parts in society and for whom, for one reason or another, life had become impossible. Some were voluble and lived in a world of fantasy, some were manic depressives of the minor kind, some were alcoholics, and some were just confused. Some bustled about the place on imaginary business and some just sat gazing into space. The saddest cases were the youngsters who had become excessive drug addicts.

Mixing with these people I suddenly realised that if I did not take a grip on things I should end up like them. I also realised that they were mostly far worse off than I was, whatever they had done. This made me try to lend a hand in a mild sort of way and to try to help those who burst into floods of tears from time to time, or sat on their beds for hours refusing to speak to anyone. I even organised a debate at which the motion was 'The Age of Chivalry is not dead'. It went quite well, although there were numerous interruptions and one of the hecklers had to be removed for using unsuitable language.

I did not remain inside for long. But that is perhaps a somewhat over-dramatic description of my position as I was allowed to leave the establishment whenever I wanted and paid regular visits to London. I had realised that it was time for me to set about picking up the pieces while I was still capable of doing so. I knew it would not be easy, but on the other hand it would be a lot easier for me than for many of those with whom I had been living. It was an experience which had destroyed the spirit of hopelessness and turned back the rising tide of self-pity which had been gaining control of me.

Meanwhile a change had come about, at least officially, in the ordering of society by the passing of the new Sexual Offences Act. I feel myself reasonably well qualified to examine the nature of that change, the reasons why it had to come about, and the effect it has had upon those concerned.

Before I turn to this examination of the whole problem as it concerns other people I will look back for a moment at my own disaster and the psychological effects it had upon me. On reading what I have written it has occurred to me that it may appear at first sight to be a somewhat devil-may-care account of what was regarded in certain quarters as a public scandal. I suppose that this may be due to the fact that it was an event which I had foreseen as a possibility and for which, in a strange sort of way, I was prepared.

As a politician I had learned to be tough and I had also been brought up to be tough which was just as well. I would not describe this as courage because I am not really certain of the meaning of courage. To those who would wish to know more about it, and to those who think they know all about it, I recommend Lord Moran's book, *The Anatomy of Courage*, which admittedly deals largely with men in battle. In it he writes: 'Courage is will-power whereof no man has an unlimited stock: and when, in war, it is used up, he is finished.' This is also true of men in peace except that in peace courage can be replenished more easily: in war the object of the replenishment may well have been liquidated or may have become a mental ruin. This, too, of course, can happen in peace.

To a certain extent the experience of war is bound to have an influence on one's approach to life, even in a semi-sedentary and semi-exposed position such as mine. All around there is death, destruction, violence and human misery, and eventually it all becomes part of living. When it is all over it brings with it a kind of immunity, or so it has seemed to me.

When something happens to a man of the sort that happened to me he is faced with the alternative of self-destruction or self-reconstruction. As I have indicated I was not afraid to choose the first, nor was I prevented from doing so by any religious convictions. I just did not think it was the way to behave which may seem rather incongruous, in view of the way I had already behaved. So I chose the second because I thought it was the way to behave and was also what people would expect in the circumstances. I know that I was right but it was not an easy road. I felt rather like the Germans must have felt when they surveyed the ruins of their country in 1945 and had to set to work to build it up again. Everything I had believed in, rightly or wrongly, had been smashed to pieces and I had to start from scratch to build it up again.

Self-degradation is not exactly the best basis for morale building: it has not the same spiritual significance as self-abasement. To have been caught in an embarrassing situation in a public place, albeit in the middle of the night, to have struggled with a policeman, to have been clamped in a cell, to have stood in the dock like

a criminal and to have been at the same time Parliamentary Under-
Secretary of State for Foreign Affairs and a Member of Parliament,
was, to put it mildly, quite an experience.

It surprises me that my courage did not run out at that moment.
I take no credit for the fact that it did not. When one considers
those who have to go through life without sight or hearing or who
are deformed or crippled because for some mysterious reason a
merciful God wanted it that way, it would not be particularly
courageous to run away from a minor handicap of this kind. Nor
would it have been particularly courageous to cock a snook at God
and become an atheist. It was a challenge which had to be met.

It would have been easier for me in those early days if the new
legislation had been passed and people had come to take a more
intelligent and rational view of the whole subject. As things stood
I cannot complain that I was ever openly insulted. It is for this
reason amongst others that I find it difficult to subscribe to the
somewhat emotional view expressed by Oscar Wilde that 'the road
is long and red with monstrous martyrdoms'. To talk like this is to
damage the case of the homosexual and to reject the validity of
the rule of law which exists for the protection of society. I do not
believe that there is anything akin to the martyrdom of men who
have died for their faith and punishment of men for committing
what was, until recently, a legal offence. To have believed this
would have been to betray my trust as a politician.

The fact that I did betray that trust was for me more serious
than what I actually did. I felt no sense of martyrdom or guilt. Not
only did I betray that trust but I also betrayed the institutions in
which I believed and the friendship of all those who had understood me to be a different person. I betrayed those who loved me
and depended upon me. Worst of all I betrayed myself. This meant
that I could no longer put such abilities as I possessed to their
fullest use. I was made to realise, although I knew it already, that
'The fault, dear Brutus, is not in our stars but in ourselves that
we are underlings.' But for me it seemed that there were no longer
any stars : only a long dark night.

5 No more jeering at Clapham Junction

Rather the scorned, the rejected, the men hemmed in by the spears.

JOHN MASEFIELD

THE problems of the homosexual in our society have been greatly increased by the attitudes of the protagonists on either side. On the one hand there have been vicious attacks, grotesque misrepresentations, and completely unfounded assertions; on the other there have been hysterical *cris de cœur*, absurd social demands and embarrassing outpourings of self-pity.

In view of my personal involvement I have not been unaware of this and I have found the examination of the experiences of others both interesting and helpful. The most important development has of course been the passing of the Sexual Offences Act of 1967 which was the result of the Report of the Wolfenden Committee, published in 1957. Ten years is a long time in which to reach a decision, but better late than never.

During the 'sixties a number of books on both the social and medical aspects of homosexuality appeared which have been objective, well reasoned and have been based on extensive research. I have studied them carefully and I have no quarrel with the majority of their conclusions although there is, not surprisingly, a certain divergence of opinion on the origins and treatment of the matter. Some of the latter have become outdated by the most recent legislation. Rather than add what might be regarded as a great deal of repetive information to this book, I have referred hereafter in the text to the authors who have, in my opinion, made the most valuable contribution. As a result of my reading I have reached the conclusion that it will not be out of place for me to make some observations as a member of this society of people which is under examination, and as one who is not in prison or under medical care.

Public awareness of homosexuality has been increased, both for better and for worse, by a number of novels, films, television plays and, since the abolition of the power of the Lord Chamberlain, theatre performances over the last few years. Things have reached such a pitch in some directions that it has become difficult to avoid forming the conclusion that heterosexual behaviour is 'old hat'. In order to restore the balance the protagonists of heterosexuality have had to resort to taking off all their clothes in public. This exhibition of general permissiveness and a desire to be regarded as 'with it', although 'it' is extremely difficult to define, has in effect done the homosexual society more harm than good. They are now in danger of being subjected to the 'back-lash' which is the result of the work of over-enthusiastic reformers, bent writers, and irresponsible promoters of public entertainment. Jokes about 'queers', 'queens' and 'pansies' which were once told in private are now commonplace : and all jokes tend to go stale.

In its present judgement society remains confused and 'the establishment' is careful not to go too far towards any actual change in its official position, although it is prepared to make outward concessions when expressing its views in order to appear progressive, which is an essentially Conservative tendency.

Although the pages of history produce a long procession of homosexuals who have occupied positions of considerable authority such as Sophocles, Julius Caesar, and a number of English kings, the name most closely associated with homosexuality in the public mind in Britain is unquestionably that of Oscar Wilde. Here again there has been considerable misunderstanding over what he actually did and why he was convicted. The knowledge that he was a married man with children would be received with astonishment in certain quarters where he has always been thought of as a roaring pansy. Until Wolfenden there was a considerable muddle in the public mind about the nature of bisexuality : whereas homosexuals clearly had to be denounced, it was felt better not to admit the existence of bisexuals. It is not without relevance to observe that people who have gone to considerable lengths to denounce the Victorians in other ways have, in the case of Oscar Wilde, adopted an almost hyper-Victorian attitude based on false reasoning and ignorance of the facts. Admittedly Wilde did himself no good in this respect by some of his remarks at his trials, nor was the publication of his unfortunate work *De Profundis* a helpful contribution either to his personal or his literary reputation. Nevertheless, in the latter case a good deal of light is thrown on the reactions of the homosexual under duress, and for me at least this makes interesting study.

One of the most general misconceptions about Oscar Wilde is that he was a perverter of youth, which even the most sympathetic regard as both a sin and an offence. This is not true. He had two sets of homosexual relationships: the one with Lord Alfred Douglas, Robbie Ross, and others who were in the same social class as himself, and the other with the rougher elements of society who appeared at his trial: private soldiers, grooms, and the like. It is true that there were a number of young men involved, but they were already in 'the trade'. This does not make his association with them any more commendable but it does remove the allegation that he was responsible for initiating them into the ways of corruption. If he did in fact say that 'he was starting the day at the bottom of a new page' it was a risky joke in the full sense of the word. If it was true it is also improbable that the young man in question learnt anything he did not know before.

There still persists the impression, which has been clearly expressed by Quintin Hogg, that the adult male homosexual is attracted to the young male adult to the exclusion of all others. This is a dangerous generalisation and is not substantiated by facts. If it were true it would have strengthened the arguments for not changing the law. The new Act does in fact protect youth, and rightly so, but the evidence is that those involved learned the practice in early youth largely from experimenting with others of the same age.

One of the most absurd observations made at the trial of Oscar Wilde came from Sir Frank Lockwood who said to Alfred Taylor, 'You are an old public-school boy. Was it not repugnant to your public-school ideas, this habit of sleeping with men?' A distinguished journalist, W. T. Stead, commenting on this piece of nonsense, wrote, 'Should everyone found guilty of Oscar Wilde's crime be imprisoned there would be a very surprising emigration from Eton, Harrow, Rugby and Winchester, to the gaols of

E

Pentonville and Holloway.' I doubt if he was ever invited to present the prizes on speech-day at any of these august establishments. Today this is one of the most telling arguments for co-education. Those who argue that co-education has similar dangers are on the verge of conceding that the line drawn between heterosexuality and homosexuality is an extremely thin one. In fact it is not one line but two parallel lines which encase the world of the bisexuals. Since I have had the opportunity of studying boarding-school co-education in action I have been intrigued to learn of the number of cases of male and female homosexuality existing together.

There were a number of other erroneous and prejudiced remarks made at Wilde's trial which have been recorded and examined by Montgomery Hyde who, both as an author and when he was an M.P., has done much to put the whole subject into its right perspective. What was said then by the prosecution was wholly excusable because it is the function of a prosecution to prosecute with every available weapon, both intellectual and emotional. The same is not true of what was said by the Judge. The judgement of the *Daily Telegraph* was that 'He has been the means of inflicting on the public as much moral damage of the most hideous and repulsive kind as no single individual could well cause.' The *Daily Telegraph* was then, as it is now, a good Conservative newspaper. I doubt whether it also reported that after Wilde was convicted the prostitutes of London danced in the streets.

These, however, were the Victorians for whom sex itself was an improper word. In such circumstances Quintin Hogg's warning of the terrible effect that the whole episode had on Lady Wilde and her children, which it undoubtedly did, are of little relevance today except in the circles in which Conservative Lord Chancellors move.

After Wilde had been sent to prison he had to come to London for his examination in bankruptcy. On the way back to Reading he had to stand on Clapham Junction station on a grey, wet day handcuffed to a gaoler. He was recognised by the public who gathered round him and jeered. What a society. No wonder the Edwardians had a reaction, although it was not in favour of homosexuals.

In gaol Wilde wrote his famous letter, *De Profundis: Epistola in Carcere et Vinculis*, addressed to Lord Alfred Douglas. As I have said, I think that this did neither him nor his literary reputation any service. Whilst it contains flashes of the true Wilde it also contains a great deal of confused thinking though this is quite understandable. The flood of self-pity is embarrassing and his remarks on the subject of religion border on the idiotic even when read by an atheist. In Wilde's defence it can be claimed that it was a private epistle written under stress and was not meant for publication. But its title, which has the characteristic of a Papal encyclical, suggests that he knew perfectly well that it would be published : and wanted it to be.

As one explanation of his homosexual conduct Wilde wrote : 'Tired of being on the heights I deliberately went to the depths in search of a new sensation.' In fact Wilde was never tired of being on the heights and it was ridiculous for him to suggest that he was. He had, as so many other homosexuals have, a '*nostalgie de la boue*'. It was just a matter of animal lust. He was nearer to the truth when he admitted that it was like feasting with panthers.

Looking back Wilde declared : 'The one disgraceful, unpardonable and to all time contemptible action of my life was to appeal to Society for help and protection.' In so far as he made any such appeal it was none of these things. The facts of the matter were that he was cornered and, as a result of personal miscalculation, was caught. Until the last he clearly thought that his reputation would see him through. As a dramatist with a knowledge of audiences and the theatre he should have known that he had no grounds whatsoever for such a hope. At one moment he was the idol of society and at the next he was a social outcast. In such situations it is no good making appeals to people who are in many cases busy covering up for their own misdemeanours. It is a simple fact of life, as well as an elementary fact of physics, that the higher you climb the farther you fall. Wilde knew this perfectly well. His so-called appeal to society was merely a shocked reaction. It was neither disgraceful, unpardonable nor contemptible : it was just pointless.

Looking forward Wilde said : 'My nature is seeking a fresh mode of self-realisation.' That was precisely what he needed to do but he never succeeded. He went on to declare : 'I have hills far steeper to climb, valleys much darker to pass through. Neither religion, morality nor reason can help me at all.' It was largely for these reasons that he failed to climb any hills. He merely sank into the slough of despond and returned to his homosexual practices. He died in Paris in obscurity and degradation. It had all been too much for him which was hardly surprising in the circumstances.

Although one can feel little but repulsion and contempt for Lord Alfred Douglas he was not all that wrong when he told Wilde: 'When you are not on your pedestal you are not interesting.' Some of what is written in *De Profundis* goes a long way to endorse that. One cannot help feeling that had Wilde restricted his physical associations to his ruffians he would have been a lot happier than he was in his emotional and extremely expensive relationship with the despicable Douglas, a public-school type of which Sir Frank Lockwood had such a high opinion.

A case much nearer to our time and one which did much to underline the necessity for action along the lines recommended by Wolfenden was that of Lord Montagu of Beaulieu and his associates, Peter Wildeblood, Kenneth Hume and Michael Pitt-Rivers. Whereas Wilde was jeered at Clapham Junction and socially destroyed there was a good deal of sympathy for Montagu and the others, partly because public opinion was changing and partly because there were aspects of the case which left some doubt as to the propriety of the way in which the charges had been brought.

Since the trial Wildeblood has written his account to which I have already referred : it is entitled *Against the Law*. What is particularly commendable about all those who were convicted is that they all had to climb hills far steeper and pass through valleys much darker, and unlike Wilde they succeeded. This in itself should be an encouragement to those in similar circumstances, although mercifully these have now been ameliorated.

Before examining the findings of the Wolfenden Committee and considering what was said in both Houses of Parliament during the passage of the Sexual Offences Bill and its abortive predecessor, it is useful to consider objectively the nature of the Homosexual Society and to reach some conclusions about it. Of particular importance are the findings of the medical profession and of the sociologists, although even in the 'sixties they were the first to admit that not enough was known about this complex problem which has far more bearing on our national life than many people realise or care to admit. The writings of Dr. D. J. West and Gordon Westwood and the researches carried out by Richard Hauser and

Michael Schofield, who is in fact Gordon Westwood, are particularly commendable and so, on a broader front, are those of Havelock Ellis and Kinsey.

I venture to quote D. J. West at some length because he has, I consider, clearly defined the whole order of the problem. In his book *Homosexuality* he states: 'Writers on the subject, even medical writers who should know better, carelessly throw out generalisations without an atom of validity. One reads that homosexuals are depraved or exhibitionists or (and this is usually from the homosexuals themselves) that they are more 'alive' and 'sympathetic' than the humdrum mass of humanity. In reality some homosexuals suffer from neurotic fears and anxieties and some are self-assured and hard as nails, some are vain and ostentatious and some are shy and quiet, some are cowardly and some are heroes, some are effeminate and some are brutes . . . A mentally defective criminal and a musical genius may both be homosexual but their character and the influences that have moulded them will be radically different.'

In fact the homosexual society is an integral part of society and it is not only absurd but stupid and inhumane to try to stamp it out and to ostracise it. Such remarks as 'there but for the grace of God go I' are just a lot of sanctimonious clap-trap and goodness knows I have had to listen to enough of them.

Anyone who has associated with homosexuals, as I have, who are both open and secretive, rough and smooth, educated and moronic, knows that what West says is true. Equally untrue are such assertions as those made by my erstwhile friend Quintin Hogg, that 'active male homosexuals are made not born'. He plunges further into the depths of nonsense when he states: 'I do not believe that this is solely or exclusively due to the fear of detection or of a sense of guilt attaching to practices disapproved of by society. It is inherent in the nature of an activity which seeks a satisfaction for which bodily organs employed are physically unsuited.' Small wonder that he can claim to be the greatest political authority on 'bonkers'.

A rather greater authority on the subject in question is Dr. West from whose work I make no apology for quoting again: 'The realistic viewpoint accepts homosexuality as a universal potentiality that may develop in response to a wide variety of factors. Neurotic fears of sex, disappointment in love, an all-male background, guilt about women: all these things may contribute and tip the scale towards a homosexual development. Thus the mere fact that a man is homosexually inclined tells us nothing about his character.'

Dr. F. A. Breach goes even further than West, who quotes him. He observes that 'In our society sexual contact between members of the same sex is considered extremely undesirable. Various social goals and ethical laws are violated by the homosexual individual but to describe his behaviour as unnatural is to depart from strict accuracy.' The number of departures from strict accuracy by people who pride themselves on the veracity of their statements would fill an encyclopaedia and a great many of them have been made by lawyers and politicians.

Since Wolfenden, and since their fling in the House of Lords and the House of Commons, many of these pundits have decided to call it a day and we have something to be thankful for in that. Without seeming to attack any particular person noted for speaking out against homosexuals, it is a well-known fact that many who practise homosexuality in secret are the most virulent opponents of it in public. It is a cheap and cowardly form of cover-plan. It is also not unknown that those who have been frustrated in their homosexual affections or rejected become vindictive in their hostility. Scorned men and scorned women have a great deal in common. There are such things as homosexual male spinsters.

The fact that it took ten years for anything to be done about the recommendations of Part Two of Wolfenden is an indication of the state of mind of society. In the end the matter had to be taken in hand by Private Members which was little short of cowardice on the part of both governments but particularly the Conservatives. There is evidence that a number of M.P.s who were active in promoting the legislation, notably Humphry Berkeley and Montgomery Hyde, were subjected to attacks by their constituency associations. Berkeley lost Lancaster in 1966 and has since been unable to get another seat. It is not altogether surprising that he has since joined the Labour Party, although not for this reason. Montgomery Hyde was told outright that 'We cannot have as our member one who condones unnatural vice'. The Irish who cannot even forget Cromwell no doubt resent the fact that Oscar Wilde was an Irishman, but they have seen fit to overlook the homosexual proclivities of Casement.

The Scots also tend to take a holier than thou attitude on the subject although they should recall that they provided England with James I and VI, a monarch whose homosexual activities did more to damage the political and social conditions of his time than those of any other sovereign, William II and Edward II included. The new Act does not run in Scotland and this made Ray Mawby ask in the House of Commons whether when a train was crossing the border at night they blew a whistle to warn those in the sleeping compartments. The Conservatives did not think this was funny; but of course Mawby was one of their working-class members so what could one expect?

Sir David Maxwell-Fyfe, a notable Scot and the hammer of the homosexuals whilst in office, thundered: 'Homosexuals in general are exhibitionists and proselytisers and a danger to others especially to the young. So long as I am Home Secretary I shall give no countenance to the view that they should not be prevented from being such a danger.' John Knox, that monumental Scottish bore, must have risen from his grave to applaud such sentiments. It was not surprising that the Conservative Party in power should have shied away from taking action in the matter with such powerful influences at work.

With such sentiments being expressed in high places it was not surprising that homosexuals should tend to regard themselves as a persecuted minority. In the case of those who were homosexuals by nature, rather than simply practising homosexuals from time to time, this was calculated to accentuate a psychological condition which was contrary to that which the reformers, on both sides, aimed to achieve.

It is perhaps understandable, although it is regrettable, that the greatest hostility towards homosexuals has been exhibited by lawyers and particularly by political lawyers. Three Lord Chancellors are on record for their vilifications on the subject: Maxwell-Fyfe, Quintin Hogg and Manningham-Buller – Kilmuir, Hailsham and Dilhorne respectively. As lawyers they have no doubt met a number of cases where the worst kind of offence has been committed by the worst type of homosexual, particularly against youth. This was due to the fact that the police felt it essential to move against such offenders, whereas they left others of whom they had knowledge to continue doing what has now been recognised as legal. It is depressing that men of such intelligence, or at any rate men whose intelligence was noted as qualifying them for one of the highest positions in the land, should pursue such a restricted and obscurantist approach.

A great deal of concern, some of it justified, has been expressed at the increase of homosexual practices since 1945. Some of this is due to the war when men had no other contacts. It has been suggested that this was carrying comradeship too far, and from some points of view it undoubtedly was. On the other hand I have read that a certain commanding officer in charge of really hard-fighting troops considered it an advantage for two men who were fond of each other to fight alongside one another as it increased their determination for mutual protection. I always regarded Montgomery's order on 'non-fraternisation' with German women when we entered the Reich as asking for sexual trouble amongst the troops, and to my certain knowledge he got it. He himself had the advantage of fraternising with God. On the one occasion that I came upon two of my men involved in this way I let them off with a caution. I would have done well to have taken my own advice to heart at a later date.

The Wolfenden Committee was set up as the result of pressure by a number of M.P.s. Although I myself was a member at the time, I took no part in this; not because I was afraid to declare my interest, although this might have caused quite a stir, but I was too much involved with other matters. Their report, which took three years to produce, was a carefully reasoned document which examined the whole subject, and also that of prostitution, objectively and recommended accordingly. It is gratifying that most of its proposals were subsequently accepted; albeit after a struggle. There was nothing in it with which any balanced homosexual could disagree. It did raise the question of the age of consent, which it recommended should be twenty-one, and that is now the case. Since then the voting age and the age of decision in everything else has been reduced from twenty-one to eighteen. After the war men were still required, if necessary, to be called up at eighteen. It is reasonable to argue that anyone with these liabilities has reached the age of consent and that the Act should have taken this into consideration.

The Act does exclude the Armed Services and the Merchant Navy from its conditions which is understandable when men are on duty, because of the dangers of enforced corruption. But it is not desirable to differentiate between servicemen off duty and civilians with whom they are mixing. The Wolfenden Committee felt that the offence of homosexuality in the Forces should basic-ally be left to the discretion of the authorities. This is reasonable although there is the danger that some will treat the matter with intelligence whilst others will not. A case has already occurred of two officers who were convicted in the R.A.F. and who were both cashiered. A more humane way of dealing with the matter would have been either to call upon them to resign their commis-sions or to have posted them to other units abroad. The Wolfenden Committee correctly observed that it was not the function of the law to intervene in the private lives of people in order to enforce any particular pattern of behaviour. That is a sound democratic principle and this is claimed to be a democratic country.

The Wolfenden Committee also dealt firmly with the subject of public opinion, a matter which is of even greater relevance today with the increasingly powerful instruments of communica-tion. It was suggested during the debate on the Bill of 1966, which failed to become law, that the reason why there had been such a delay in implementing the Wolfenden proposals was that public opinion was against them and that they were in advance of their time. This was a typical Conservative argument and was an indict-ment of R. A. Butler and Henry Brooke who had slavishly fol-lowed in the Maxwell-Fyfe tradition. The Wolfenden Committee had summed up this aspect of the situation very succinctly: 'We have to consider the relationship between the law and public opinion. It seems to us that there are two over-definite views about this. On the one hand it is held that the law ought to follow be-hind public opinion so that the law can count on the support of the community as a whole. On the other hand it is held that a necessary purpose of the law is to lead or fortify public opinion.' That is an entirely appropriate statement for a non-Parliamentary Committee to make but it omits one important consideration which is the duty of the Member of Parliament in carrying out his functions.

It is the politicians who make the law. It falls upon them to give a lead to the nation. If they are not prepared to take action on any particular issue because they think it will be unpopular, despite the fact that they know it is in the public's interest, they weaken the democratic system which it is their responsibility to maintain and strengthen.

What, in any event, is public opinion? The performance of the professional 'public opinion' agencies at the General Election of 1970 shows that it is an inconsistent variant. If the House of Commons is prepared to abdicate its undoubted position as the true representative of public opinion because it contains the elected representatives of the people, then the day of the morons is about to dawn. Some people think it has dawned already in a society which is infested with inane chatterers on the box and radio, irresponsible journalists and asinine demonstrators for idiotic causes, whose daily language is prostituted with confrontations, escalations, explosions, and the like.

I would be making the same mistake as the extremists for the cause of homosexuality if I were to express my emotional reactions to the speeches made on the various occasions in the House of Lords and in the House of Commons. It is not, however, possible to avoid remarking that the weight of intelligence was on the side of the homosexuals. I say this without prejudice against my former colleagues. There has always been a dangerous Conservative tendency to avoid reform until it has become inevitable and often when it is too late. They are constantly reminded that concessions ruined Louis XVI and they can almost hear the rumbling of the tumbrils. It was also noticeable that, with very few exceptions, those who spoke in the House of Commons on the Conservative side were from the back benches although the Party was no longer in power.

In a typically puerile speech the late Cyril Osborne declared that he had evidence that Roy Jenkins, who has since been criticised as the champion of the permissive society, was supported by a number of members of the Government and he gave their names. It was not an undistinguished list and for those who were in doubt it was an argument against his own case as was also the fact that he himself spoke against the Bill. The speech of William Shepherd who sat in the House for a very long time without recognition was just grubby. Dr. David Kerr accurately described his oration as 'one long string of claptrap'. The speech of Sir Cyril Black was sickly. Collectively they make depressing reading for any Conservative, even those who disagree with the Act.

One strange statement by Shepherd concerned Richard Hauser

who wrote a highly intelligent report on *The Homosexual Society*. He quoted him as saying that he knew of no minority among which self-pity and self-righteousness were so rampant, nor of one which was so lacking in a sense of values outside its own circles and no minority so bereft of loyalty to its country. This is either a misrepresentation or a misquotation. There is nothing in Hauser's book so far as I can see to suggest anything of the sort.

The debate in the House of Lords on Lord Arran's Bill makes far better reading although nothing much was said that had not been said before. Lord Queensberry made it the occasion for his maiden speech which was extremely appropriate in view of the action of his forbears in the case of Oscar Wilde. If amends were needed it did much to make them. The former Marquis must have turned several revolutions in his grave.

The Viscount Montgomery of Alamein delivered an oration which was very much in keeping with the pontifical messages he was in the habit of sending to his troops. During the war politicians in the Forces were seldom a great success and professional servicemen who have subsequently entered politics have been even less successful. It is true that on this occasion Montgomery spoke with rather more authority than on other occasions as he was dealing with military matters as opposed to uttering fallacies on foreign policy and political leadership. Concerning his ability to command there can be no question. How far he was really in touch with the men he commanded apart from making a spectacle of himself and handing round cigarettes is another matter. He relied for his information on a group of arrogant and waspish young men who darted about the place making a general nuisance of themselves. They were known to those who had to deal with them as 'Monty's minions', and so they were.

It was inevitable that Montgomery should turn to the issue of the moral fibre of the nation being undermined by homosexuality in high places or amongst those in authority. In this he showed himself singularly lacking in his knowledge of history and particularly Greek and Roman history. In view of his outstanding book on the British Army it is more probable that he chose, like other old men, to forget. I doubt very much if that highly successful commander, Julius Caesar, would have agreed with him. It was fortunate for Montgomery that the House of Lords was not in the same frame of mind as the Senate who put paid to his distinguished predecessor, but not because of his homosexuality.

Montgomery's argument that the men would have no respect for their officers if they knew that they were going to bed with one another is highly questionable. I think they would have thought it funny in certain cases but most of them would not have cared twopence. On the other hand they would have thought it wrong for an officer to go to bed with one of his men and would have objected strongly if they themselves were punished for homosexual offences, which many of them committed, if they knew that their officers were getting away with it. Lord Montgomery ended his speech by demanding that the Bill should be hit for six. That is hardly the language to be used in discussing a serious subject but it was indicative of the speech and the mind of the man who made it.

The House of Lords provided Lord Kilmuir with an opportunity to restate his well-known philosophy all over again. He did it well but added nothing to it. He was particularly concerned with 'buggery clubs' and 'sodomite societies'. I must confess that he was better informed than I am. I have never come across either, nor have I ever been asked to join one. There is no evidence that since the passage of the new law there has been any increase in such organisations otherwise I am sure I would have heard about them. In any case they are not permitted if their activities extend to orgies and to brothel facilities. With that I am in full agreement as it is an element of segregation which runs counter to all processes of rehabilitation which, where they are feasible, are highly desirable.

Lord Brain, with whom I was later to have professional dealings, made a valuable contribution to the debate in which he endorsed the note in the Wolfenden Report made by Dr. Curran and Dr. Whitby. Most relevant was his statement 'Sexual behaviour is a spectrum. At one end are the normals, the heterosexuals, the large majority of the population; at the other end are the hard-core homosexuals, a very small percentage. But in between there are gradations of people who are in some sense both, perhaps married and with children but with homosexual tendencies which may, or may not, be given overt expression.'

He went on to say: 'There is another danger to which the latent homosexual, if I may call him that, is exposed. He may succeed in controlling his homosexual impulses until something diminishes his normal self-control. This may be an illness such as depression or thickening of blood-vessels; or self-control may weaken as he grows old or even as a result of taking alcohol and then the previously latent homosexual tendency may become apparent.'

When I went to see Lord Brain I had not read his speech but I told him without any reservations what had happened to me and why. On his advice I had a complete medical check-up with my friends at University College Hospital where I had been taken when I was seriously ill in 1958. Lord Brain did not write a detailed report about me but had he done I suspect it would have read something like this:

'This man has been subject to heavy mental stress and to psychological pressures arising from frustration and deprivation and resultant social isolation. He has sought relief through alcohol which has diminished his powers of self-control and weakened his judgement. He is a homosexual with a limited heterosexual capacity: in fact he is bisexual with a homosexual bias. He has not reacted favourably to treatment, mainly because he does not seek to be changed. Some of it has been unsatisfactory and he has had access to sedative drugs which, mixed with alcohol, have had a damaging effect upon him. His physical condition is capable of cure but he will remain a homosexual and there is nothing to be done about that.'

Baroness Gaitskell made an important contribution to the debate and her final exhortation has bearing on what I have written on the subject of Parliament and public opinion. 'Let us try to influence public opinion, this body of men with its experience, its knowledge and its ability to think clearly.' The General Election of 1966 interfered with the processes of both Humphry Berkeley's and Lord Arran's Bills. It remained for Leo Abse to begin all over again and no one could have done it better. He was assisted by the fact that the Conservatives had been heavily defeated and the atmosphere in the House was less reactionary on this score. It would be tedious and unproductive to examine the passage of the final Bill through the House of Commons. Nothing new was said. Everything that could have been said, and a great deal which would have been better left unsaid, was on the record.

At last on July 27th, 1967, the Sexual Offences Act received the Royal Assent. A long period of misery and fear was at an end for many people. To say that the social stigma and ostracism were also at an end would be to exaggerate, but at least there were a few streaks of light in the sky which had for so long been overcast.

A highly satisfactory result of the new legislation has been the removal of blackmail as an instrument in the hands of homosexual prostitutes. Blackmail is rightly regarded as one of the most evil of all crimes. Used by the homosexual it undoubtedly increased his activities and lowered his moral character, such as it was. It also increased homosexual practice in general because men who were not normally addicted to any extent found it a lucrative pursuit.

There still remains the risk of blackmail for those in positions of authority and in such places as the Foreign Service where they could become security risks and were likely to lose their jobs if their activities were disclosed. Owing to the change in the law on this count it is now possible for the blackmailer to be reported without fear of subsequent reprisals by the authorities.

But there will always be some who will prefer to pay up rather than risk a public scandal. The danger is even greater in the Foreign Service where the price to be paid is not money but secret information. This makes the screening process all the more important but, as I have shown, this is not as simple as all that because bisexuals who may have the occasional lapse are not so easy to detect. I never met Vassal, although I knew something about him, but it always surprised me that no one in the service seems to have suspected him, including the highly intelligent Sir William Hayter under whose eye he came in Moscow. The only way round this problem would seem to be to make it plain that the punishment for a homosexual relationship will not involve dismissal if it is admitted, whereas it will if it is not.

A final word on the subject of the new Act was spoken by Lord Arran who said: 'I ask one thing and I ask it earnestly. I ask those who have, as it were, been in bondage to show their thanks by comporting themselves quietly with dignity. This is no occasion for jubilation; certainly not for celebration. Any form of ostentatious behaviour now, or in the future, any form of public flaunting would be utterly distasteful and would, I believe, make the sponsors of the Bill regret that they have done what they have done.'

He was right. It is encouraging and a justification of what has been done, that nothing of the sort has occurred.

6 Towards 'Risorgimento'

*Man is not made for defeat. Man can be destroyed
but not defeated.*

ERNEST HEMINGWAY

WHEN you have fallen off a mountain you can, once you have
regained consciousness and recovered from your concussion, look
back and judge events in perspective and without emotion. If you
have not become a mental and psychological cripple, and this can
easily happen, you can also look around and survey the scene and
try to pick up the bits. If you have sufficient courage and determination you can look ahead and face the future, however dark the
prospect. All these things I have endeavoured to do, not entirely
with success, and I have recorded them as a warning and perhaps
as a help to others.

I have described in some detail my personal experiences in the
realm of homosexuality which some may consider deplorable and
others regard as an embarrassing admission of weakness. I have
also examined in less detail what has been done and said on the
subject over the last decade. As we now enter the next decade I
think it is not inappropriate to study the reactions of the homosexual society now it is not, at least officially, under the same pressures, and also to study the reactions of the community as a result
of the adjustments that have been made. From what I have written
it must be clear that this is not an academic review and I trust it
will not be regarded as a biased one.

As I have said earlier, homosexuality has been associated in the
public mind with Oscar Wilde and the association has, to a large

extent, been a confused one. I do not agree fully with the view expressed by Laurence Housman in a message on the occasion of the unveiling of a plaque at Wilde's old residence in Chelsea. He wrote: 'His unhappy fate has done the world a signal service in defeating the blind obscurantists: he has made people think.' Nor am I, as I have declared, enamoured of Wilde's own declaration, 'The road is long and red with monstrous martyrdoms.' This is the sort of language which puts homosexuality on a plane with religious persecution and to do that is to invite the sort of antagonism which it is desirable to avoid. It also encourages homosexuals to regard themselves as special people and to develop an unjustified superiority complex which is, in effect, an inverse inferiority complex.

Montgomery Hyde, a personal friend and former colleague in the House of Commons, has done, in my view, a far greater service to society in general and to homosexuals in particular in his admirable and authoritative book, *The Other Love*. He is not unnaturally kinder to the memory of Oscar Wilde than I am, as he has himself written a very capable account of both the trials. He, like Wilde, is also an Irishman. He has also given a very full account of the history of homosexuality in this country since the Normans, who were much more addicted to it than school history books disclose. School history books declare, nevertheless, that England owed a considerable debt to her conquerors and there was no sign of weakening of the national fibre under their rule; in fact exactly the reverse was the case. This is no justification for those homosexuals who glorify their position by citing men of distinction in society and men of creative genius who have made their mark on history and have escaped the fate of Oscar Wilde and others.

I am not a psychologist and therefore I do not feel qualified to explain why it is that such people become so involved. I have referred already to that *nostalgie de la boue* which undoubtedly affected Wilde. There are also the various well-known forms of perverted behaviour which are common to many so-called normal heterosexuals of which self-degradation is one. Although I have rejected Wilde's claim that he was tired of the heights for the reason that he gives, I think it is true that he was attracted by the idea of an altogether opposite type of society to the one to which he was accustomed. An examination of this highly complex condition would, I believe, show that in the main it is no more complex than various conditions of heterosexuality. The association of Edward II and Gaveston had much in common in carnal terms with that of Charles II and Nell Gwynne. In these cases the influence of the inferior element on the public conduct and authority of the superior was far more deplorable than the private sexual activities involved. It follows from this that similar associations between men who are not in positions of authority and who are not required to set an example of public behaviour are socially of less significance. When important people choose to ignore this, it is right that they should pay the price which society demands of them; what is dangerous is the situation which arises if such people are in a position to avoid that payment and, consequently, society is exposed to general perversion. As Havelock Ellis has remarked, 'morals are in perpetual transition'. And that, undoubtedly, was one of the main fears in the minds of those who opposed homosexual reform.

When Montgomery Hyde's book, *The Other Love*, appeared in the spring of 1970 the reviewers were, to a large extent, in agreement that this was an accurate and informed account of the position of homosexuals in Britain over the years and a reasoned assessment of their position before and after the most recent legislation. There was one contribution which appeared in *The Yorkshire Post* which was more in the nature of an article than a critique. It was written by a practising psychiatrist and contained a number of statements which appear to me to border on the insane. The object of the author was to sound the alarm that homosexuality was on the increase. It proclaimed :

'Greater tolerance has converted the latent and repressed homosexual into the active practitioner. With increased permissiveness his sense of guilt in relation to society is inevitably lessened. There are many in whom homosexuality remained at the level of fantasy who have translated their dreams into action.'

This is, of course, exactly what the opponents of the Bill said would happen. It should be noted that there are no facts or figures given to sustain this assertion. A further assertion sheds some light on the author whose professional status has enabled him to claim anonymity.

'A certain type of invert', he writes, 'is saturated with spiritual pride and convinced of his cultural superiority over others. In the course of my clinical experience I encountered many homosexuals

F

for whom the heterosexual was essentially a person of coarse fibre incapable of artistic appreciation or creation. . . . It is an accepted litany among cultured homosexuals that the production of works of art is almost their monopoly.'

Unlike the author of this article, I am not a practising psychiatrist but I regard this contribution on his part as a generalisation of the sillier sort which does his profession no good. It is to be noted that he refers in the past tense to his experience and from this one would deduce that he was no longer practising when he wrote this diatribe. It is a belated and ill-conceived attempt to put the clock back. If he was practising in Yorkshire and his statements are true of the majority of his homosexual clients then I am sorry for Yorkshiremen but there is little evidence that that extremely robust county is peopled with such a collection of psychopaths. A more courageous writer would have given the exact figures and signed his name.

Leo Abse in reviewing Montgomery Hyde's book observed that 'The main purpose of the reforming Act was not to remove criminality from a discreet homosexual relationship: that was incidental. The real purpose was to shift society away from the punishment of homosexuality.' That is a very reasoned analysis by a man who, more than most, should know what he is talking about.

Three major advances have been achieved on behalf of the homosexual society as a result of the new legislation. First, the threat of blackmail has, in the main, been removed.

Secondly, the punishment of imprisonment has been abolished except in cases where men break the new law which is designed to protect society. As Leo Abse himself said so appropriately, 'We all know that to send a homosexual to an overcrowded male prison is therapeutically as useless as incarcerating a sex-maniac in a harem.' Indeed we all knew it and had known it for years but we had done nothing about it.

Thirdly those homosexuals who would wish to be cured are more likely to avail themselves to access to the medical profession, which is now more understanding, without the same fear of making a disclosure of criminality. Not that there was any danger of the doctor disclosing a medical secret but no man likes to admit to a criminal offence especially if he is a highly respected member of society.

A further help has been a change in the attitude of the police.

Allegations have been made that, in the past, the police have gone out of their way to obtain prosecutions against homosexuals. Examples have been given, and Wildeblood discloses one particularly unpleasant case of the police acting as *agents provocateurs.* It is also a fact that on certain occasions when a homosexual has reported a case of blackmail to the police it has ended up with his being prosecuted himself. There have also been cases of 'bent' policemen resorting to blackmail. I have had no personal experience of any such behaviour and my own dealings with the police at all times, both under happy and unhappy circumstances, have been such as to convince me that most of these accusations are unfounded. In principle it is highly undesirable that relationships between the police and any element of the public other than criminals, should be fraught with mistrust and hostility. The effects that this can have upon society have been demonstrated by events in the United States, and in France in particular. It is now a practice in certain quarters to attack the police who have an extremely difficult task in maintaining law and order in the face of student and racial outbursts. There exists in this the undertones of an attempt to identify the actions of the police with those of a police state. It is not difficult to calculate from what sources such suggestions emanate.

The new legislation has relieved the police of the kind of witch-hunts that Maxwell-Fyfe and his zealous lieutenant Nott-Bower, whose family were friends of my family in Richmond, encouraged them to pursue. I am certain that for many of them this was a most unwelcome duty. It was an activity which was calculated to increase the social insecurity and sense of persecution amongst homosexuals which, in view of their numbers, was hardly likely to stabilise society. It had in it exactly that sort of destructive element to which the opponents of homosexual law reform declared themselves to be opposed. Despite accusations to the contrary, homosexuals, even when pursued under the Maxwell-Fyfe régime, have not displayed collectively any violent hostility towards the police, whom they have recognised as merely doing the duty imposed upon them from above. I myself have certainly never had any inclination to react in such a way. On those occasions when I have visited the House of Commons I have always been treated by the police in particular with the same courtesy as if I were still a Member of Parliament.

I must admit that this experience has coloured my judgement of a state of affairs about which my knowledge is restricted. I have been informed by those who have practical experience that there is still a tendency in certain police forces to pursue homosexuals and young constables in search of promotion find this a rewarding activity. I am told also that the practice of training *agents provocateurs* in the force still continues. The figures of arrests do vary considerably from district to district, which lends substance to this accusation. This underlines the necessity for a common policy and indicates the undesirability of leaving the exercise of judgement to the discretion of individual chief constables.

One of the most important contributions of the Wolfenden Committee, although perhaps not immediately recognised as such, was to define the nature and practice of homosexuality and to draw a clear line between the complete homosexual and the man who practices homosexuality as well as having heterosexual inclinations. Once this was accepted, and for some people it was extremely difficult to accept in the light of past prejudices and beliefs, the road was clear to educate public opinion. If the law had been designed to deal only with that small minority of out-and-out homosexuals so clearly defined by Lord Brain the case for passing it would have been greatly weakened although it would still have been valid. As soon as it was realised that many apparently normal people with whom one mixed every day and who might belong to the golf club or the rugger club were liable to prosecution as a result of their secret activities a far more liberal and understanding view of the situation began to be taken. Parents, in particular, became aware of the fact that they might suddenly discover that their sons were involved.

Although it may appear to be an odd and controversial assertion I believe that the problem of the complete homosexual is far more simple in its social connotations than that of the bisexual. The former belongs by nature to a clearly defined group which, in the main, does not seek to mould itself into the structure of normal society. The main harm which this group does is to itself, and there are many resultant cases of loneliness and despair, and a sense of being outcast, which lead to mental disorder and to suicide. But the causation and the conditions are largely definable and although they present a serious medical problem, it is not a major problem for society itself because society as such is not directly involved and tends, in any case, to veer away from it rather than to be infected by it. Admittedly there is a danger to youth in the formative years, but this danger has been reduced by the recognition that bisexuality and homosexual practices are no longer completely and inescapably associated with this group. It is now possible to conceive of homosexual friendships with what the Americans would term 'regular guys' without being labelled as 'queers' and damned for life. Whilst it is right that the age of consent should be a qualifying factor it does raise, once again, the question of what that age should be.

Generally speaking, though it is always dangerous to speak generally in this context, the group of absolute homosexuals is easily recognised although less so in an age of long hair and drug addiction. I often wonder if, from time to time, there are not cases of accidental homosexuality owing to mistaken sexual identity.

Reports, such as those by Hauser, Westwood and Schofield, show that the bisexual in the past has been much more worried by what has appeared to him to be a disease largely because it has been condemned as a criminal offence. The same also applied to homosexuals who were not recognisably so and were, one can reasonably assume, not incapable of becoming bisexuals. I quote two examples which give an indication of their state of mind.

One man said, 'When I found out I was a queer I nearly went mad. I hated my body because I thought it was filthy.' Another declared, 'If they knew about this where I work they would get rid of me pretty smartly. They always say that all homos should be castrated.'

The moralist will consider that this was the way it should be and that both men were displaying a proper acceptance of the evil of their condition and that any steps to change such a reaction, such as to suggest that it was not evil, were wrong. But the relevant fact is that this acceptance did not change the condition of either man and merely produced a damaging guilt complex which could have the effect of driving them irrevocably into the arms of the absolute homosexuals because of their fear of the opinion of the heterosexuals. There is a good deal to be said for the Chinese proverb, that 'It is better to satisfy the body than to discolour the mind'. Needless to say I agree with this sentiment.

It is difficult at this point in time to make any precise assessment of the reaction of society as a whole to the change in status of the homosexuals in their midst if such a phrase can be regarded as appropriate. Dr. West wrote, before the change took place, 'however enlightened we become as individuals we remain prisoners of our culture'. To some extent the conception of our culture has also changed and one hopes that he, and others equally qualified, may see fit to make a further study.

It is certain that such remarks as that of Lord Winterton, who said that the Oscar Wilde case was a moral purge, and of George V, who observed that he thought that such people as homosexuals shot themselves, would today be received with astonishment or derision. But the 'establishment', not unnaturally, has been reticent about expressing itself on the subject when such cases arise : there is no particular reason why it should not be so : it usually keeps silent. Various attempts have been made in the past to weigh up social attitudes to the subject. Here again generalisation has proved to be a dangerous measurement.

Peter Wildeblood went so far as to say in his book *Against the Law* : 'The homosexual world knows no such boundaries [class] which is precisely why it is so much hated and feared by many of our political die-hards. The real crime of Lord Montagu, for example, in the eyes of some "society" people was that he became "acquainted"—on no matter what basis—with a man who (to quote the prosecuting counsel) was infinitely his social inferior.' This was an over-simplification of the facts which it was understandable that Wildeblood, after what he had suffered, should make. Although I would not accept either the fear or the hatred, he was certainly right on the social issue so far as the Montagu case was concerned.

Since the Montagu case there has been a very considerable change in the strata of society not unassociated with six years of Labour Government : that is all to the good. Even so, Harold Wilson did not go out of his way to give a special party for redeemed homosexuals at No. 10 Downing Street nor would it have been appropriate from anyone's point of view for him to have done so. If he had had it in mind I could have supplied him with an interesting guest-list and it would not have consisted solely of Labour supporters. That would have appealed to him.

Oscar Wilde, rather in the same vein as Wildeblood, observed that 'the poor are wiser, more charitable, more kind and more sensitive than we are'. That again is an emotional over-statement which, in any case, is now out of date. Hauser quotes a working-class man as saying that if his son turned out to be a homosexual he would 'shoot the bastard'. It is not, in fact, true that there is any marked class difference in opinions on the subject of homosexuality. Nor is it true, for social reasons, that there are any clearly defined barriers in its carnal practice although there are more when it comes to what could be defined as true-love associations, and these are dictated by class distinctions. Very few people live with their prostitutes, as opposed to their mistresses, although it is sometimes difficult to tell the difference. It is also true that the more extensive type of homosexual relationship, involving living together, is more temporary than similar types of heterosexual relationship. Homosexuality is a more fickle relationship than that of heterosexuality. In its defence, it can be far less damaging than the latter and does not cause such problems as unmarried mothers and illegitimate children of which society, so intolerant of homosexuals, has plenty.

It has been stated in the past that certain professions and trades attracted homosexuals: this was understandable because they were more freely accepted and no questions were asked. Actors, fashion designers, waiters, hairdressers, and shop-assistants were most commonly named. Politicians were clearly not on the list. I do not know whether there has been any great change in this tendency. From my observations I suspect not.

Suggestions have also been made that some sporting activities have a high quota of homosexual participants accounted for by the physical qualities required. Boxers, all-in-wrestlers, footballers and jockeys have been mentioned, though with what degree of truth I do not know. I have had no experience in any of these fields. I must admit to being slightly suspicious ever since a man I met in a pub told me that muscular rugby footballers were very much to the fore as a homosexual attraction. Rugby is a game with which I have been associated all my life and I have never detected even a glimmer of any such suggestion. When I told my informant that I played in the second row of the scrum he went away delighted and convinced of the truth of his theory. I found the idea extremely laughable; my only fear now is that the Rugby Union, who love altering the laws, may feel it desirable to add this to the list of offences.

I do not think any useful purpose would be served in describing the sexual activities of homosexuals. For those who wish to satisfy their pornographic appetites there are a number of books, novels and photographs available in such places as Soho, where similar provision is made for heterosexuals, at excessive prices.

I have already referred to the increase of homosexual presentations in the world of the theatre, television and the films. Most of these have set out to present an intelligent and sympathetic picture of aspects of the homosexual society and have not concentrated upon the lurid aspects for box-office purposes. I have seen most of them and, with a few exceptions, I have found them interesting and, in some respects, helpful. Probably the most accurate and the most difficult to present was Mart Crowley's *Boys in the Band*. Had it been acted without sensitivity it would have been an embarrassing vulgarity; as it was, it was both moving and informative. The *cri de cœur* of one of the main characters 'Show me a happy homosexual and I will show you a happy corpse' was a good line for theatre, but, coming from the character it did, it was only a half-truth uttered after a large number of dry martinis. My evening was enhanced by two American ladies who sat next to me and who thought they had come to see a jolly musical. They left after the first act.

A number of writers have involved themselves in the homosexual world and in many cases they have done it with accuracy and taste. There are of course notable exceptions. I do not commend for the reading of the young the works of Jean Genet or of de Sade. In saying this I run the risk of their rushing at once to the bookshops, especially now that these authors are available in paperbacks. I do not condemn such books in the sense of literature; in fact the reverse is true. But in dealing with their subject they make *Lady Chatterley's Lover*, which was banned when I was young, seem like a Christmas pantomime. But even Christmas pantomimes have changed so much these days that it will not be surprising to see Robinson Crusoe having an affair with Man Friday before the decade is out.

These are aspects of the permissive society which, as I have said, could do the cause of the homosexual great harm if continuously carried to excess, but there is no more danger in them than in similar exercises in the heterosexual sphere.

The question of the age of consent is controversial and requires to be examined again with a view to the amendment of the Act. Now that eighteen is accepted as the age of responsibility it is logical that it should also apply to homosexual practices. On the other hand heterosexual activity is legal at sixteen. It is contended that young people are now far more advanced than they used to be and this is generally true, although some of the advances are highly dubious in their effect both on the young and on society.

The Dutch Government, as a result of a report prepared for the Minister of Social Affairs and Health at the request of the Minister of Justice, has recommended that Parliament be asked to reduce the age at which it is possible to have a legal homosexual relationship to sixteen. In reaching this conclusion the committee who made the report were influenced by the answers to a number of questions, of which the most important were that there is no danger of seduction of minors above the age of sixteen by homosexual adults; that homosexual experiences by minors aged over sixteen does not give rise to a permanent attachment to a homosexual way of living; that a young person's heterosexual development will not be adversely affected by homosexual associations between the ages of sixteen and twenty-one. These conclusions require careful consideration not least of all because of the possible closer relations between this country and Holland in the future. It seems unlikely that this will enter into the discussions on Britain's entry into the Common Market, which are difficult enough as it is.

Another matter which requires consideration is the restriction of the association of homosexuals in public. This is admittedly equally controversial but the present legislation is so worded as to make it possible to proceed against homosexuals on the mere basis of assembly which suggests that, unlike heterosexuals, they cannot meet one another without immediately wishing to commit the sexual act. Social workers who feel that getting certain homosexuals together may help to stabilise them run the risk of being accused of procuring two people to commit the homosexual act together which is, of course, the very reverse of their intention. Similar dangers are faced by those who think that it is in the interests of the homosexual society to establish clubs along the lines of those which exist in Holland. Admittedly both courses are open to abuse but the present situation retains the atmosphere of hostility on the part of society and the feeling of being victimised for the homosexuals. Until the law is amended, and with so many heavy problems pressing on government, this is unlikely to happen in the near future, a great deal depends on its intelligent application by the authorities and that, in turn, depends, to a great extent, upon public opinion.

Much needs to be done in educating public opinion so that homosexuality ceases to be regarded on the one hand as an exciting practice which every 'with-it' male should experience or, on the other, as an evil menace which will destroy the moral fibre of the nation. Those who would seek to work for this, and I count myself amongst them, must avoid emotional histrionics or they will feel the backlash of an outraged majority.

It is extremely difficult to define public opinion with absolute accuracy and it is also difficult to say precisely who creates it and why, from time to time, it suddenly changes. Those responsible for opinion polls will admit this, particularly after their experiences at the last General Election. What is clear is that the views of the majority are largely dictated by the minority and that minority is mainly composed of those who control and operate the communications industry, of which I have some experience. Political, social and religious leaders must concern themselves with this instrument of power if they are to lead rather than be led. Because, to a considerable extent, they themselves are the source of authority they are in a strong position to do this but, for the same reason, they are extremely vulnerable and this applies particularly to the politicians.

Walter Lippmann, who is a considerable pundit on this subject, has written: 'Where mass opinion dominates the government there is a morbid derangement of the functions of power. This derangement brings about the enfeeblement, verging on the paralysis, of the capacity to govern. The breakdown in the constitutional order of things is the cause of the precipitate and catastrophic decline of Western Society'. He wrote this before the emergence of television. At this particular time, the 'telecrats', the new-style journalists, exercise a powerful influence over the minds of the people who have developed an addiction for 'the box' which has gravely damaged the erstwhile power of the Press; this largely accounts for the closure of some newspapers and the parlous plight of others which once considered themselves invincible. This power can be, and has been seen to be, extremely dangerous under certain circumstances when opinions have been expressed on political and social issues by people who have no actual responsibility for conducting affairs.

Those who are concerned with educating public opinion on the subject of homosexuality must study this medium with great care just as they must concern themselves with the Press. This is no longer a time for the sort of controversy which took place when homosexual law reform was before Parliament. No good purpose for instance would have been served by challenging the hysterical nonsense written by the 'Practising Psychiatrist' in *The Yorkshire Post.* But a careful statement of the homosexual case by authoritative people from time to time will not come amiss. In the main, journalists and 'telecrats' are neither hostile nor reactionary. There are, of course, exceptions such as the venerable Scottish patriarch, John Gordon who delivered an onslaught at the time of the Montagu case. He wrote, in typical vein :

'An emotional crusade seems to be developing to legalise perversion and even to sanctify perverts. Perversion is very largely a practice of the too idle and the very rich. It does not flourish in lands where men work hard and brows sweat with honest labour.

'It is a wicked mischief destructive not only of men but of nations. Those who are raising sentimental howls in its defence would do Britain a better service by lending their support to stamping it out'.

That contribution to the discussion can best be described as ill-informed poppy-cock. Fortunately John Gordon cannot be said to be a power in the sphere of influencing public opinion.

Hauser has recorded a number of opinions expressed by the public in the early 'sixties which indicate the depth of ignorance about, and the extreme enmity towards, homosexuals. I quote three which are almost unbelievable as coming from citizens of an educated democracy.

'These ―― should all be castrated. I would be glad to do it myself. Otherwise why not kill them?'

'I think every father and mother who produced a queer ought to go to prison for letting them grow up like that.'

'Queers and Communists are both undermining our Western civilisation. They ought to be eradicated'.

Those responsible for such remarks are of the type who undoubtedly gave their support to the Nazi movement which was, at the same time, riddled with homosexuals of the worst type. But there is little doubt that they would all class themselves as men of rectitude. To what extent such views still prevail it is difficult to assess but it is only ten years since they were prevalent.

Before the passing of the new Act, Mr. R. A. Butler observed to a deputation which went to see him that there was no case to proceed because the public had not shown its feelings in the matter. But the public had never been asked. There is little doubt that had the situation been in reverse and it was planned to introduce a law designed to institute the sort of proceedings against homosexuals which did in fact exist, there would have been considerable opposition to it – from probably over seventy per cent of the community. But to assume this is to make a supposition of the same order as that made by Mr. Butler in his determination to do nothing. Henry Brooke adopted a similar attitude to that of his predecessor, and took shelter behind a public opinion which had never been analysed. One suspects that both he and Butler were afraid that they might go down in history as the Homo Secretaries. Such an analysis of public opinion is now required if a correct solution is to be found for the problems which still exist both for the complete homosexual and for the bisexual.

I find myself in agreement with His Honour J. Tudor Rees and Mr. Harley Usill who have written in the book edited by them and entitled *They Stand Apart* that 'there are two parties to be considered, society and the individual, each having inherent rights which have to be safeguarded'. Since they wrote this the law has conferred new rights upon the homosexual and this has to be taken into consideration.

Whereas it is difficult to produce a clear definition of 'public opinion' as opposed to 'private opinion', so it is equally difficult to produce a clear definition of 'public morality' as opposed to 'private morality'. A simple answer is to state that anything which is contrary to the law is a breach of public morality. But it is a fact of life that you cannot legislate to make people moral. Again, problems are posed by religion. The Christians believe that certain acts are immoral but agnostics and atheists reject their conclusions.

Despite the fact that Britain is officially a Christian country there are probably more atheists and agnostics about than there are prac- tising Christians.

It has been my experience on occasions, and I have recounted one, that no one is capable of being more un-Christian than the professional Christian, especially when he sees himself as a modern St. Michael casting out the devil from society. Since I have seen some of them at work I have reached the conclusion that had I been in the Colosseum at the time I could well have been on the side of the lions. Some Christians, for instance, are able to reconcile their anti-semitic views and conduct with the fact that the founder of their faith was a Jew. Or at least He saw fit to assume that nationality whilst on earth.

In the light of these observations it may seem both strange and illogical that I should, in the midst of my difficulties, have become a Roman Catholic. The cynics will say that it was a form of escap- ism, and perhaps it was. I will not deny that in the process there were moments when I was tempted to go in the opposite direction. I have found it not without its humorous side that since I joined the Church in 1965 it has been involved in a state of controversy. The student of history will recognise that this is not for the first time; but these present disagreements differ from former contro- versies in that they involve the laity and lower echelons of the priesthood to a far greater extent. The Catholic Church is con- fronted by public opinion in a way in which it has never been seri- ously confronted before. In the manner in which it has reacted there is a serious danger of this developing into a flight from authority.

For one who has crossed the border and has seen the processes of so-called participation at work this is disturbing to say the least of it. For those who were brought up as Catholics it must be bewildering and I have seen a certain amount of bewilderment upon faces around me. This is not the place to become involved in this argument. It only affects me personally since I turned to Catholicism because I saw in it, as many others have done before, a stability and authority of which I felt myself to be in need. To find that authority challenged and that stability in danger of being weakened was alarming in the first instance. Now I feel that it presents new problems which I could help to solve if anyone wants me to help, but the Catholic Church has always been nervous of enthusiastic converts, and with some reason.

Neither the Catholic Church nor the other religions have had much to say on the subject of homosexuality, with the exception of those Bishops who took part in the debate in the House of Lords and Canon V. A. Demant who was a member of the Wolfenden Committee. In the past the position of the Catholic Church was very positive and homosexuals were condemned to death when the ecclesiastical courts had power over them. Today it would seem that it is still a subject about which Christians don't speak, but I may be wrong. I have never raised it with any Catholic priest and no Catholic priest has ever raised it with me. Maybe that is my fault. To have fallen like Lucifer is one thing, to be treated like him is another.

Lord Arran was unquestionably right in warning the homosexual society to avoid any demonstrations of jubilation as a result of their liberation from one aspect of their bondage. But it would be a mistake to believe that that is the end of the story. There remains for them and for those who are concerned with the problems they present, and with which they are beset, the psychological and the social issues.

Having studied with some considerable care the various reports on the subject I have been astonished at the objections, and in certain cases the hostility, with which those who compiled them were met in various quarters. All this work was done in the 'sixties, most of it after Wolfenden but before the new Act. It is to be hoped that these attitudes may, by now, have changed. These reports have largely been concerned with the problems of the complete homosexuals many of whom have not been capable of a complete cure nor have some of them desired it.

The reactionary approach by elements of the medical, and even of the sociological, professions was surprising in view of the fact that the operation was designed to help them in dealing with cases which they clearly found difficult and sometimes insoluble. Perhaps that was the reason. Havelock Ellis, writing before the war, observed: 'But there can be little doubt that we shall gradually break down the false notions and the rigid attempts at social prohibitions which have caused so much trouble and confusion in the sexual history of our recent past. In doing so we shall purify our spiritual atmosphere and our moral code by removing from it prescriptions which were merely a source of weakness.'

It was no wonder that the old gentleman in the Carlton Club was horrified by what he read: if indeed he understood it. Today the rigid attempts at legal and social prohibition have been broken down, and it has taken an unconscionable time for it to be done, but many of the false notions still remain – some of them in the minds of the homosexuals themselves.

Relevant to this, and in a sense more advanced even than the statement by Havelock Ellis, with which he clearly agreed, is the proposition by A. L. Worbarst who stated: 'Homosexuality has always and everywhere existed. It is one of the intersexual conditions within the natural and inevitable range of variations. We may possibly find ourselves on the correct road if we act on the theory that any sexual deviation which has given satisfaction without injury to a particular individual must be considered normal to that individual.' As Alfred Taylor said at the Wilde trial, 'Where there is no harm done I see nothing repugnant in it'.

The acceptance of that position goes a long way to assist the complete homosexual in his psychological condition: it is of equal assistance to the bisexual. But it is not a position which is easily accepted by society and therein lies the real difficulty. Dr. West has underlined this by pointing out that tolerance towards homosexuals is not the same as encouragement. He has also pointed out that male homosexuals are men first and deviants second. It is the refusal to accept either of these propositions by people whose views accord with those of the late Lord Winterton who, one generously hopes, the Lord above is now preserving, which has made the road so long for the homosexual. The coast is now clear for those who have the professional qualifications to deal with homosexuals without feeling that they are in some way consorting with criminals. Those who retain such feelings, and they are undoubtedly few in number, are no credit to their profession.

As I have indicated I consider that the problem for the bisexual is more difficult and, to an extent, I am biased in making this assertion. Bisexuals have none of the obsessions of the homosexual in their relationships with a society which has no reason to suspect them unless they are particularly indiscreet or unless they are caught. Whereas the fallen homosexual merely returns to his own, the fallen bisexual finds himself barred from normal society. That is a considerable punishment.

For me it meant my exclusion from the Conservative Party to

which I had given the best years of my life and a considerable
part of my energy. When you have politics in the blood you
cannot just drain it out and take a transfusion of something else
unless you are very talented. I have therefore remained a keen
spectator of politics having found it impossible to break with this
interest, although I have been told by innumerable people that that
is what I ought to have done. I am sure they are right in principle
but in practice it is not so easy.

Dr. West has said that 'the suggestion of tolerance runs counter
to a very common constellation of emotionally determined attitudes.' It is not difficult to see, and events have proved this to be
the case throughout the debates on homosexual reform, that such a
constellation resides in the Conservative mind. This made my position doubly difficult. And it has not changed much over the years.

I have, therefore, become an onlooker of the political scene; the
sort of touchline politics which never, in the past, appealed to me.
What has made this even more galling has been the fact that
the Party is now pursuing policies which, if properly carried
out, should remove many of our present discontents. In its present
mood it has become both more progressive and more democratic.
That is a process in which, as I hope I have shown, I have always
believed.

The most unhappy period in the Party's post-war history was
that which was spanned by the leadership of Alec Douglas-Home;
it was the end of a tired Government and the beginning of
a confused Opposition. It was one of the typical injustices of
politics that Douglas-Home was held, at the time, to be largely
to blame. It has been said of him that he is the greatest gentleman
in politics today; I would go along with that. Whether that was
the essential requirement for the man who had to take over from
Harold Macmillan is debatable. The circumstances of his appointment were hardly auspicious. These will always feature in my mind
as the 'Blackpool Follies of 1963' when the great mass of active
Conservative Party workers found itself in the presence of a top-
level grab for power with the final decision being made by a man
from his sick-bed who was mainly accessible to right-wing members of the Party and who, in any case, had made up his own mind.
People who are ill in bed are hardly in the best condition to make
important decisions and, unless they become delirious, unlikely
to reverse decisions.

It is easy enough to criticise but it is more constructive to suggest what would have been a better solution. The two main contestants were, by right, Butler and Quintin Hogg. Butler had been passed over for Macmillan largely on the grounds that his conduct over Suez had proved that he had not the necessary fire in his belly to pull the Party through its crisis. There is little doubt that Macmillan continued to hold that view and when a question of his own successor arose he ruled out Butler. He may have been right. I think he was wrong in the prevailing circumstances but under the conditions then operating, but which, largely due to this whole affair, have now been changed, his view was decisive. Lord Hailsham who, under a Labour Government, had not been permitted to renounce his peerage, was now in a position to do so, and was ready to return to the Commons. But he had overplayed his hand in the eyes of the rank and file with his bell-ringing and bathing-trunks appearances. More seriously his colleagues were never quite certain whether his emotions might not overrule his considerable intellect at some vital point and involve them in another Suez. The experience of history proves that either candidate would have been suitable for the task, but the advice of history was ignored.

At that moment it was too early for the members of the 'Class of 1950' to be considered. There is evidence that Harold Macmillan had been grooming Maudling, Macleod and Heath for stardom and Macleod indicated in his account of the whole affair which he wrote in the *Spectator* that he had not at that point decided which it ought to be. In view of Macmillan's ingrained belief in supporting those who were particularly loyal to him, which admittedly broke down on the occasion of the 'night of the long knives', I would suspect that he favoured Heath. If it had been a matter for the Party to decide at that point I think Maudling would have won. But to have involved any of the three with Butler and Hailsham also in the fight would have been asking for serious trouble in the Party when unity was essential as the next General Election was not far off.

Alec Douglas-Home was the one man about whom there was no immediate controversy because he had not been considered as a serious contender. It was when he accepted the leadership that the controversy broke out; but it was then too late because he was also Prime Minister and any attempt to reverse the decision would have totally wrecked the Conservative Government. The decision of Macleod not to serve under Douglas-Home finally put paid to his chances of the leadership. Maudling who with Macleod and Enoch Powell had tried to prevent this development took the view that his duty to the Party was to sink his differences. Heath was never involved and that undoubtedly strengthened his position.

When Alec Douglas-Home took over, the Conservatives had been in power for nearly thirteen years. As in 1945 people were beginning to get bored with the old faces. It was time for a change. The performance at Blackpool was hardly calculated to inspire confidence in the country. Nevertheless the General Election was only just lost and it was clear that Harold Wilson would have to go to the country again as soon as he felt that the time was ripe. Before that happened Sir Alec Douglas-Home had resigned. His resignation was prompted by what was tantamount to a revolt of the younger Conservative back-benchers who were influenced very much by the same arguments as were used by the opposition to his appointment. Had he not been so much of a gentleman he would have told them to jump in the Thames or would have used even stronger language. But he too was influenced by much the same arguments which had caused him to accept the leadership.

So Edward Heath became the Leader of the Party and they proceeded to lose the next General Election by a resounding majority. As I have recorded, he was soon in trouble and the Party began to have second thoughts about Sir Alec Douglas-Home. He, in turn, became the idol of the rank and file partly because they had a conscience and partly because he had behaved impeccably. This did not make things any easier for his leader but that was not his fault. One thing was clear to anyone but a political idiot and that was that the Conservatives could not afford to have a third leadership crisis in fourteen years and four leaders in fifteen. But there were a lot of political idiots around.

In fact the Labour Government of 1964–70 did a great deal to assist the Conservatives. Harold Wilson, despite his undoubted political ability, generated over the period an almost universal mistrust even amongst his own followers. A great deal of nonsense was talked about 'character assassination' by the Press and on television but it would be far more accurate to call it *hara-kiri*. Most significant was the emergence of the Labour Government as a bureaucracy with the clearly stated intention of ordering the lives of the people. This would have been more acceptable if the process had been successful. As it was the cost of living continued to rise, restraints on initiative in industry increased, government spending went up without any visible results except that there were more office blocks filled with more and more civil servants, the housing programme fell short of its stated targets, unemployment rose, particularly in the mining industry, and, worst of all, taxes went up, pursued by wage demands which were not accompanied by increased productivity. It was an exhibition of failure on almost every front at home whilst internationally Britain's influence continued to decline and although this was almost inevitable it was put down to the ineptitude of the Government, which was demonstrated by Harold Wilson's theatrical débâcle on H.M.S. *Tiger* and George Brown's grotesque behaviour as Foreign Secretary.

The Conservatives proceeded to win a record number of by-elections with increasing majorities and as the General Election approached nearly every major local authority came under their control. It is therefore difficult to account for the sudden swing towards Labour, according to the pollsters in May which, whatever he may have said to the contrary, made Harold Wilson decide on a June Election. There were, in my opinion, two factors which, had they been seen in their present perspective, could have led to a massive Conservative victory. The first was the leadership question and the second the policy issues outlined at Selsdon Park. The Conservatives themselves had done a good deal of damage on the first score by what was scarcely concealed disloyalty and scepticism. Harold Wilson seized this as the main chance, for which he always had an eye, and turned his attention to promoting a personality battle on the American Presidential model. But Heath was neither to be daunted by the one nor inveigled by the other. He shouldered the full responsibility for leading the Conservative campaign and behaved with courage and integrity in the face of a storm of personal abuse and with a party which looked at one time as if it was losing its nerve. As a result he moved to a position of strength which invested him with an almost complete authority as Prime Minister.

The Conservative Party declaration of policy at Selsdon Park made it clear that the next Conservative Government, like the

Conservative Government of 1951, was going to be very different to its predecessors. In view of the record of the Labour Government it was in a strong position to do this. It promised to put an
end to the age of interference and to establish a proper relationship between Government, industry, and the people. Edward
Heath summed up the position in the Party Manifesto 'A Better
Tomorrow' when he wrote: 'So it will not be enough for a Conservative Government to make a fresh start with new policies. We
must create a new way of running our national affairs. This means
sweeping away the trivialities and the gimmicks which now
dominate the political scene. It means dealing honestly and openly
with the House of Commons, with the Press and with the public.'

In June 1970 the public either did not understand these policies
or they regarded them as typical election promises which would
not be carried out. In any case they doubted if Edward Heath
was the man to carry them out: after all if a number of Conservatives were going around saying he was not the right man to be
their leader it was not logical to argue that he was the right man
to be Prime Minister. During the last week of the campaign Harold
Wilson overplayed his hand and, owing to the balance of payments
figures and the unemployment figures, the public decided that an
attempt was being made to fool them. But they only decided by a
very small margin.

It remains now to be seen whether the Conservative Government under Edward Heath will have the ability and the courage
to carry out its intentions and whether the policies outlined at
Selsdon Park are workable. I personally believe that the concept of a
new style of government makes sense but it will only make sense in
the eyes of the people if the major problems presented by the state
of the economy and by industrial relations are solved. Added to
these will be the question of joining the European Common
Market which will become a national issue in 1971. If the Conservatives do not succeed on all these fronts they will be in dire
trouble by 1972.

A disturbing aspect of the situation is that the Labour Party
appears to have no effective alternative but to bring in a more
extreme form of Socialism. For this they could have a mandate if
all else failed. It is not beyond the bounds of possibility that the
Conservatives would be forced to forestall this by making another
appeal to the people; but the danger in this lies in the fact that it

could be interpreted as an admission that the conception of long-term government was not working out. It could also lead to a very sharp conflict which could divide, rather than unite, the nation. Under either circumstance the future of democracy would be in jeopardy. A very heavy responsibility now rests upon the shoulders of Edward Heath and his colleagues which will require all their resolution and the complete loyalty of the Conservative Party. To achieve a new government is one thing, to achieve a new society is another.

For anyone in my position this is a state of affairs which is fraught with an element of emotion. To see those who were once my friends and colleagues fighting a battle for a cause in which I fully believe and to be able to do nothing to help is frustrating. Some time back I thought that the time had come, in view of what had been done in Parliament, when I might return from the wilderness to lend a hand. But I was told when I asked if it would be possible for me to be reinstated as a member of the Carlton Club that some members had said if that happened they would resign. This did not surprise me in view of their expressed opinions. That was not the only rebuff I was to receive at the hands of the Conservative Party; it is clear that for me, on that score, a better tomorrow is not envisaged. I regret that, but, being an experienced politician I quite understand. It is not, however, a happy augury for those who have to pass through the dark valleys and climb the steep hills; it will not be surprising if some of them get lost on the way.

I would hope that most of them will not encounter the same obstacles and I would hope too that there will be more people who are now prepared to help them on their path. But the need still exists for greater understanding and to achieve this more has to be done to extend the scope of the studies that have so far been made. They are commendable but, in view of the nature of the problem and the number of people involved, they are inadequate. To those who would conduct quiet revolutions I would observe that humanity comes first and there are no exceptions to that rule. Compassion is not enough.

Epilogue

Quod scripsi, scripsi.

PONTIUS PILATE

THERE is a peculiar tendency amongst people to think that a new century, a new decade and even a new year is bound to bring about some sort of change in their lives. A simple examination of history proves, if proof were needed, that this just is not so. Nor is there any valid reason why it should be. It provides, nevertheless, for the journalist, the advertising man, and even for the politician an admirable opportunity to use such words as new, progressive, evolutionary and even revolutionary without being called upon to explain themselves if nothing of the sort transpires.

The arrival of the 'seventies has proved no exception. They have been hailed as a new decade which will be dramatically different from the dangerous 'thirties, the exciting 'forties, the changing 'fifties and the permissive 'sixties. If someone drops an H-bomb this may well prove true. From a less sombre point of view the passage of the new legislation concerning homosexuals at the end of the 'sixties does make it reasonable to hope that in this particular area of human relations the 'seventies may be a new decade of constructive advance.

There are clearly two sides to the problem: the attitude of society towards the homosexuals and the reaction of the homosexuals towards society. From what I have written in this book I hope I have made it obvious that there is scope for considerable progress to be made and that there are also grave dangers that, as a result of mishandling on the one side and misconduct on the other, the position could deteriorate.

As Dr. West has correctly observed, 'Homosexuals are so numerous they cannot all be serious misfits or outstandingly peculiar.' But society, by its treatment of homosexuals in the past, has tended to make them into misfits and to create more 'boys in the band' than was either justified or reasonable. There are, of course, misfits amongst homosexuals just as there are amongst heterosexuals. It is no solution to use such expressions as 'stamp them out – castrate them – shoot them' or to say of homosexuality that 'one may as well condone the devil and all his works'. There was a time, under the eminent Victorians, when people who were mentally deranged were treated with the same sort of inhumanity. It was assumed that for some inexplicable reason, they were the product of sin and an offence in the sight of God. Havelock Ellis, a man before his time even in the 'thirties, declared that 'we should not be ashamed of what God was not ashamed to create'. Some professing Christians could do well to note such advice; the attitude of such people makes me agree with Frederick William Rolfe, the only man who actually created a Pope, who said, 'I loathe not the Faith but the Faithful.'

The homosexual society, for their part, would also do well to bear in mind what Havelock Ellis has also said concerning them : 'No one is entitled to seek his own good in any line of action which involves evil to other persons.' In speaking of the homosexual society I would underline once again the dividing line between the complete homosexual, the sexual deviant, who has a positive aversion to the heterosexual act and, in extreme cases, to any form of heterosexual association and the bisexual who, from time to time and for various reasons, such as alcohol and heterosexual stress, becomes involved in homosexual practices.

For the former, what is required is a more profound and intensive medical and sociological examination and a greater degree of public tolerance and compassion. For the latter all he needs is a quiet and intelligent acceptance of a condition of the mind which is not a form of insanity and an accompanying mode of reserved and unobtrusive conduct. Both must realise that homosexuals are men first and deviants afterwards and must behave accordingly.

Just as the heterosexual pederast is rightly punished in the interests of society, although he may be a seriously sick man, so must the

homosexual who perverts men who are under the age of consent, whatever that may legally be declared. There must be no breach
of this on the grounds that the law, as it stands, is not justified by
physical facts.

Mr. Douglas Brown, discussing Montgomery Hyde's book in
the *Daily Telegraph*, has wisely written: 'Policing in the past at
least saved our society from the embarrassment of too public a
manifestation of emotional attraction between males. We must now
build up, as other nations have, a tradition of self-imposed discip-
line for the comfort of the majority.' In building this up the leaders
of society have a major part to play. The politicians have already
made a considerable contribution, although some of their remarks
have made one wonder why such men were ever given the power to
control other men's lives: most of them no longer have. The
sociologists, the psychiatrists and the medical profession in general
have much to do. It is to be hoped that it will not be said of their
work, as it was of Kinsey, that the world would be cleaner if they
stuck to their rats. Finally the men of religion who have been
singularly uninspired in this field, as they have in many others and
have consequently lost their following, must make up their minds
and, in doing so, they should recall that for them, above all others,
humanity comes first.

The members of the homosexual society have their part to play
so that they do not take advantage of their new-found freedom to
cause offence to people who, however obscurantist they may seem,
are sincere in the moral position which they have taken up and are,
after all, in the majority. Tolerance is needed on both sides and
because, in the past, it has been absent on the one that is no excuse
for it to be rejected now by the other.

It is understandable that those who work to improve the lot of
homosexuals should feel that progress since the passage of the
new legislation has been extremely slow. What is happening now
should, however, be considered against the background of what
happened before. Prejudices die hard. Admittedly this is no
excuse but it is a reality which has to be accepted with patience
and which fully justifies the continued activities of those concerned. This is not exactly encouraging but it is the normal experience of the reformer.

The case is strengthened by the fact that society concerns itself
to a much greater extent with alcoholics, drug addicts, excessive

gamblers, mental defectives, unmarried mothers, prostitutes, ex-prisoners and neglected children. For the homosexual there is no such concern and assistance is left to such voluntary aid as can be provided by the Society for Sexual Reform and the Albany Trust whose resources are slender indeed. So long as this attitude persists the homosexual will continue to suffer from an inescapable alienation which creates a social neurosis which makes the task of integration into normal society excessively difficult and, in many cases, impossible. This is a rejection of Wolfenden and to reject Wolfenden now is to reject the principles upon which the new Act is based: and that is political and social nonsense. It will be interesting to see whether the 'quiet revolutionaries' of the Conservative Government of 1970 will do anything about this. For a bachelor Prime Minister this could present difficulties but for 'quiet revolutionaries' such difficulties should not be insurmountable though this does not mean that they will be able to be silent about them.

The identification of the homosexual society with the concept of the permissive society is inevitable, particularly at the present time. There are, moreover, aspects of the permissive society which are highly undesirable such as the rejection of authority in any form and the discarding of all standards of morality. These are essentially extremist minority positions which intentionally mistake licence for liberty. Socially such positions are untenable and damage the more liberal elements in what is a progressive approach to the future. If they are allowed to prevail they will inevitably produce a reaction which would be equally damaging in its restrictive processes. In that reaction the new tolerance towards homosexuality would suffer if the homosexuals by their behaviour became involved. The younger element in the homosexual society should walk warily.

It remains now for me to sum up my own position in this whole matter. Having set down all the circumstances of my downfall this will not take long. I have examined the main conditions of homosexuality and I do not find in myself anything particularly unusual. All the normal, or I suppose I should say abnormal, ingredients are there. I believe that homosexuals are born and not made and it is obvious that there are in some men the elements which, when circumstances arise, such as the lack of a father, an over-solicitous mother, an intense male friendship, cause them to deviate. All these things applied to me as they have done to many others. I am not ashamed nor am I resentful of my condition: I accept it.

I have tried to avoid sentimentality in what I have written whatever may be my personal feelings in the matter. I agree with Oscar Wilde that 'sentimentality is merely the bank-holiday of cynicism'. I am aware that many others will not agree. In avoiding cynicism I have, I realise, been less successful but I make no apology to those about whom I have been cynical. When much of the fun has gone out of life and happiness is too seldom on the agenda one is entitled to grasp what little remains just for the kicks. I have, I trust, not tried to make excuses for the inexcusable nor have I blamed anyone else, not because I am magnanimous but because there is no one else to blame, which is an irritating position for a politician to be in. Because politics are in my blood I still count myself a politician and when I study the present Conservative Government I think I can say without undue arrogance but with some offence that I believe I am one of the best politicians they haven't got. Nor do I find the view from the scrap-heap particularly entrancing.

I have read with great sympathy and interest that remarkable book *My Father and Myself,* by J. R. Ackerley with whom I find that I shared the same doctor, the amusing and colourful Harry Wadd, who had the questionable distinction of saving my life when a careless nurse had upset a saucepan of boiling cocoa over me. The experiences which I have recounted are by no means as intriguing or personal as his, which is disappointing. It is a beautifully written book and not without courage. What does astonish me is that he should have had any doubts about his father's homosexuality, concerning which he embarked upon a considerable search. I can only assume that it was due to a mixture of filial affection and a wrongly held belief that anyone who could have associations with so many women could also have associations with men, despite the fact that Ackerley's father was in the Household Cavalry: *pace* Harry Legge-Bourke. Simon Raven knew better, as he reveals in *Boys will be Boys.* Ackerley paints a picture of a bisexual which repays study by those who do not understand and firmly believe that Jim at the office is not that sort of a chap but a 'regular guy'. Good old Jim! Ackerley did not make the mistake that I did of breaking the eleventh commandment. Had he done so he would almost certainly have been sent to prison where he would have made a lot of new homosexual friends. As he was not in public life he would not have found the punishment so hard to bear. But between the lines one detects he was not a happy man although he must have managed to appear so. And that is how it should be, otherwise it is boring for one's friends. He found happiness in the end with Tulip, his Alsatian bitch. It is not the sort of conclusion to which I aspire, although some animals are much nicer than people, and his book about Tulip makes better reading than many autobiographies: mine included.

I do not agree with the description of T. S. Eliot's Elder Statesman who 'in becoming no one he became himself'. About some so-called statesmen I will not mention it is certainly true. If, in fact, it is true of me, although I am no statesman, I can't say that it gives me much satisfaction nor anyone else I suspect. I hope, however, that with my personal experience for what it is worth, (in financial terms five pounds for breaking the St James's Park Regulations), I have been able to make a reasoned analysis of a subject about which, as I said in the prologue to this book, there is both ignorance and prejudice. If in this, and in other ways, I can help confused and unhappy people and correct misinformed ones then, I suppose it can be argued, it has not all been in vain. Like J. M. Ackerley's father, 'I hope people will be kind to my memory'. If they are not at least I shall not be around to care.